Shaping Wood
A New Woodworking Approach

Shaping Wood
A New Woodworking Approach

Douglas Hackett

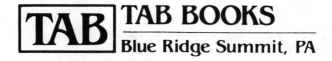

TAB BOOKS
Blue Ridge Summit, PA

FIRST EDITION
FIRST PRINTING

Library of Congress Cataloging-in-Publication Data

Hacket, Douglas.
   Shaping wood : a new woodworking approach / by
Douglas Hacket.
      p.   cm.
   Includes index.
   ISBN 0-8306-3937-3 (h) ISBN 0-8306-3936-5 (p)
   1. Woodwork. I. Title.
TT180.H29   1992
684'.08—dc20   91-33696
                             CIP

TAB Books offers software for sale. For information and a catalog, please contact
TAB Software Department, Blue Ridge Summit, PA 17294-0850.

Acquisition Editor: Stacy Varavvas-Pomeroy
Book Editor: April D. Nolan
Director of Production: Katherine Brown
Page Makeup: Wendy L. Small
Cover Design: Holberg Design, York, PA
Cover Photo: Courtesy of the producers of Wolmanized® Wood. Project designed and built by Archadeck®.

Contents

Introduction

Designing and building unusual projects in my parents' house and backyard was a favorite pastime for me while growing up in Morristown, New Jersey. Any scrap wood, plastic, or wire my father brought home from his plastics plant immediately became part of my latest contraption.

Summer jobs working in the plastics factory and high school and college courses led the way to a career teaching Industrial Arts. The highlight of my teaching experience has been the unique projects made by my students—including recumbent bicycles, wooden canoes and boats, and set designs for the drama club. Other unique projects were made by my students using a method of woodworking I began to experiment with in college.

Through an open-ended assignment that one of my professors gave, I became involved with designing and constructing sculpted wooden furniture. It turned out to be a very profitable homework assignment. After two of the projects were completed and graded, I placed them on consignment in a nearby art gallery. About a month later, the gallery owner called and said he had sold them for $2,000. The commission I received from that sale seemed like a million dollars at the time. The matching set that sold so quickly consisted of an adult-sized rocking chair and a floor lamp, both sculpted from laminated sections of birch plywood (both projects are described in this book).

But there are more than just financial advantages with this type of woodworking when compared to traditional furniture-making techniques. No experience is necessary to create quality pieces because there is nothing complicated about the process. Investing a lot of money for large power tools is not necessary because all work is done with small portable tools. All of the operations can be accomplished outside on days when the weather is clear, so you do not even need an indoor work area. In addition, the design possibilities are unlimited, and developing a new project is fun and easy.

I decided to write this book one day while I was shopping for books to use in my classroom. I noticed that the existing instructional woodworking books on the market really do not focus on helping the reader complete a project. Confusing plans, pages and pages of unnecessary information, and difficult techniques were just some of the common traits I noticed in the books that would prohibit beginners from completing the projects offered. After looking through at least 30 books on woodworking, I left the store empty-handed.

Everything I've learned about shaping wood and every method I have developed over the past 11 years is covered on the following pages. Each project includes a list of tools, materials, and supplies you will need for that project, and over 150 photos throughout the book illustrate the construction stages from start to finish. The text is written for project-oriented people, busy people, experienced woodworkers, and even children. In fact, many of the operations for the larger projects can be accomplished with no electric tools, so even young children can safely help adults cut, glue, shape, and sand.

Much of the wood left over from the larger projects is suitable for the smaller projects (such as the children's toys, vases, and small lamps). The latest tools useful for this type of woodworking are demonstrated in the step-by-step sequence, and one easy-to-master technique is used for all the projects.

One final observation: While photographing my niece and nephew for this book while they worked on their projects, their enthusiasm made my tasks much easier and more enjoyable. The ease with which they handled the various steps reinforced my conviction that anyone can make the projects I have chosen for this book. At one point, my brother stepped out of his house and asked, "How are they doing?" It suddenly occurred to me that this was most likely the first woodworking project his children had ever been involved with. Their projects came out great! I know your sculpted woodworking projects will turn out great, also.

How to use this book

Before you begin any woodworking project, you should always try to obtain an overall understanding of the technique, tools, and materials required. For this book, that means reading chapters 1-3 thoroughly before beginning any other project in this book.

Chapter 1, *The Technique*, provides you with brief descriptions of and recommendations for the most appropriate tools and materials to use, as well as an overview of the method itself. This chapter also includes important instructions on how to enlarge the plans in the book so that you can work with them effectively.

Chapter 2, *Safety*, is a section you should not overlook. Safety is essential for any type of woodworking project to be successful, and it is especially important when working with power tools. In addition, if you plan to have children involved in the work, be sure they, too, understand general safety rules.

Chapter 3, *Building the child's rocker,* is a complete, step-by-step, start-to-finish example of this unusual technique. You will find it much easier to make any of the other projects in this book if you first read and review this chapter.

Once you have carefully read these three chapters, you can go on to try your hand at any other project in this book. Each project in chapters 4-17 includes its own tools and materials list. You'll want to consult this list before you begin a project so you can be sure that you have all the tools you need on hand and that you won't run out of anything before you complete the project. Also be sure to take a look at the project photo, so you'll have an idea what your finished piece should look like.

Finally, just give it a try. You will no doubt find this unique approach to woodworking both easy and satisfying, and the projects you create are sure to be functional works of art.

CHAPTER ONE

The technique

The woodworking technique used to make all of the projects explained in this book has many advantages. Not only are the time and equipment requirements minimal in comparison to traditional methods of furniture building, but large table saws and band saws are not used, so very little floor space is necessary.

What You Don't Have to Do

You don't have to have years of woodworking experience to complete a quality piece of furniture using this method. One easy-to-master technique is used for all the projects in the book, large and small. Advanced woodworking techniques, such as making French dovetail joints or compound cuts, are not required either.

You also don't have to interpret measured drawings filled with confusing dimension lines and hidden lines. The plans provided are straightforward, and chapter 2 gives you detailed instructions on how to enlarge them from the book's page.

After enlarging the pattern to full size, you merely trace around the shapes to transfer the design to the wood. With the smaller projects, you will start "shaping" the wood almost immediately, as these projects do not involve stepped laminations. Even with the other furniture projects, though, very little measuring is necessary. You will need to make a mortise-and-tenon joint for the rockers, but all that involves is cutting four *mortises* (slots) and four *tenons* (tongues). Most of the joint is "hidden," so a large tolerance is incorporated into the design.

You don't have to be an artist to sculpt the contours for the projects. There is, however, a degree of "eye work" required when removing wood to create a natural flow of grain line and tapers. With traditional forms of woodworking, the machinery or cutter controls the amount of wood removed from the stock material. During the shaping stages for the projects in this book, the amount of wood removed is controlled by you, the woodworker. Consequently, no two pieces are exactly alike.

This technique is a combination of woodworking and sculpture, but don't let that intimidate you if you can't draw—I can't, either. Rounding and tapering the various sections is actually easy and fun. You start with an original block of material that can be very boring to look at—much like working with clay. When you see the globs of glue and stepped laminations of wood before shaping, you will find it hard to believe they could ever be transformed into a beautiful rocker, lamp, or table. Once the project is completed, however, you'll find it even harder to believe how easy it was to create a unique piece.

Designing new projects is easy because you can make any piece of furniture using this technique. Matching sets of three pieces or a whole roomful are possible. I've often thought it would be fun to customize the interior of a van with this style of woodworking. It also would be easy to transfer the techniques learned for constructing wall panels, shelving, closets, and cabinets.

Where to Work

I made my first rocker while living in a small apartment. I did the gluing and finishing work on a tiny kitchen floor, and the dusty work with portable electric tools outside of the apartment. An extension cord, which ran through my bedroom window, was my source of power.

Any location with a 120-volt outlet and a small area to keep materials dry and warm is sufficient for the construction of even the largest project (the adult rocking chair). You can use a small, portable generator if permanent electrical service is not available, but be sure to use some type of Ground Fault Circuit Interrupter (GFCI) with your power tools, especially if they will be used near water or outside. Some types of GFCIs are installed merely by plugging them into the existing outlet, and they are not very expensive. However, always consult a certified electrician before installing any electrical safety devices and for a general safety check of the existing service.

Tools

All the projects are made with portable electric tools and hand tools. You only need a few for each project, and these are listed in the tools and materials lists for each chapter.

A variety of power tools are used to cut, shape, and sand, and many of these are pictured in the following photo.

Generally, the more you spend on any one tool, the faster you will be able to complete your project and the longer that tool will last, but don't worry if you don't have an extensive selection of power tools. Quality projects are possible using very inexpensive tools.

Top row (left to right): 15-amp right-angle grinder; router with   template guide and ¼-inch straight cutter; 10,000 rpm right-angle grinder. Middle row: saber saw; hand drill with drill guide attachment; hand drill with pneumatic sander; two handmade sanders. Bottom row: Small die grinder; Soft disc pad; Drum sander; Large die grinder.

As a struggling student working on my first rocker, I purchased the least expensive tools to get the job done. For cutting, I used a light-duty saber saw. I could not afford clamps, so for gluing during the laminating and assembly operations, I used piled cinder blocks for the needed pressure. I also used common-purpose rope, twisted very tight with a stick, to apply pressure. I was able to shape around the tight curves with a 14-inch half-round wood rasp, a woodworking file, and some old-fashioned "elbow grease."

Renting all the tools you will need is something to consider if you plan to make a limited amount of projects. One weekend I rented a heavy-duty right-angle grinder to shape the larger surfaces. I used a 7-inch rubber backing pad with a #16 hard- backed sanding disk with a grinder. It was well worth the $20 for the time I saved.

For sanding, I purchased an inexpensive orbital sander and an electric hand drill to use with sanding drums of various sizes. I also used a soft disc pad with adhesive-backed sanding discs.

As I began to make furniture to sell, I upgraded my equipment and woodworking techniques. For cutting I switched to a better-quality saber saw and to using a router in conjunction with a Masonite template. The router is equipped with a ¼-inch carbide straight cutter and a template guide. Shaping is much faster now with the use of a lightweight high-speed right-angle minigrinder, equipped with a 4½-inch rubber backing pad and an aluminum-oxide-fiber sanding disc. For shaping the tight areas, I use a die grinder equipped with a ½-inch rotary rasp. For sanding curved areas, I use a pneumatic sander connected to a hand drill.

For cutting the wood there are a few alternatives. Tools I have used are routers, saber saws, and lightweight, benchtop band saws. The portable band saws are very handy for cutting the small projects and small sections of the furniture. The router or saber saw is used in the early stages of operation. Both tools are comparable in terms of cutting speed, but a top-of-the-line saber saw will cut faster than an inexpensive router, and vice versa.

Use Table 1-1 as a quick reference for the power tool options. Making sturdy and functional furniture without a huge initial investment in tools is one of the advantages of this type of woodworking.

Table 1-1
Power Tool Chart

Process	Good	Better	Best
Cutting Masonite template	Coping saw	Saber saw	2 tools in conjunction: saber saw and a portable band saw
Cutting wood	Coping saw	Saber saw	3 tools in conjunction: router, saber saw, and portable band saw
Clamping	Twisted rope and cinder blocks	Handmade clamps or C clamps	Handscrew woodworking clamps
Shaping wood	Large wood rasp	Small right-angle grinder and a die grinder	3 tools in conjunction: die grinder, large and small right-angle grinder
Sanding	Orbital sander	Random orbit sander	4 tools in conjunction: pneumatic sander, small right-angle, drum sanders with hand drill, random orbit sander

Materials

A wide variety of materials are suitable and fun to work with. For the smaller projects, such as the lamps or model boats, you can use any of your favorite woods. I usually use butternut, cherry, walnut and pine for these projects. I like the natural color of these woods, and they are easily shaped with an electric grinder.

For the furniture, plywood is the best type of wood to use. Indian birch plywood or even construction-grade plywood will work, but I recommend solid-core plywood, ⅝-inch thick, with 12 layers of hardwood. The many layers add strength, and they look like a natural grain pattern in the finished piece. This type of plywood is commonly used for concrete forms in the construction industry, Formica desktops, and sports equipment.

In addition to the strength in this plywood, any voids in it are filled with wooden boat patches during manufacturing. This permits you to sculpt without exposing large holes or loose knots.

All of the matching furniture pictured in this book is made with birch plywood, which is imported from the Baltic region and sold under different trade names. I have used plywood made of alternating layers of birch and fir, which was easy to sculpt. However, plywood made with all birch is easier to finish and more durable, and a natural, more consistent color is easier to achieve. This type of plywood is readily available and less expensive in the large port areas, but you should be able to purchase it through your local lumberyard.

I've purchased plywood from large wholesalers in Massachusetts, Pennsylvania, and New York. The sheet sizes I've always used are 4 by 5 or 5 by 5 feet. (It doesn't matter which direction the grain is running.) I have had no problem buying small quantities of plywood from the large wholesale distributors, and some even offer a credit plan. The yellow pages of your phone book will help you locate lumberyards in your area that carry or can order the lumber you need for your project.

Enlarging the Plans

The plans, which are found with each project, can be enlarged in several ways. For the smaller projects, you can use a photocopier that has enlarging capabilities. Another method, which works well with the larger plans, is to use a transparency of the plans on an overhead projector to project an enlarged view directly onto the template material. The third alternative is to enlarge the plans with grid paper.

This method requires patience, but you can achieve an accurate set of patterns using it. I used this method to reduce my adult-size rocking chair plans down to the dimensions for the child's rocker. Most art supply stores sell large sheets of grid paper with 1-inch squares, but it is also easy to draw your own.

The following sequence shows how to make a grid pattern to enlarge the plans for the child's rocker. Use the same procedure for all the plans (one square = 1 inch in all the patterns).

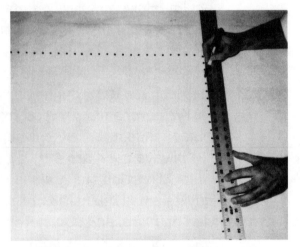

Step 1.
Use a ruler and a pencil to measure and mark dots 1 inch apart along the four edges of a 24-x-24-inch piece of paper. The dots must be congruent so the vertical and horizontal lines you draw in the next step are perpendicular.

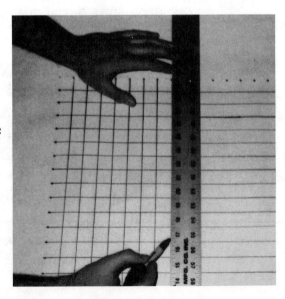

Step 2.
Use a straightedge to connect the dots to create a grid pattern with 1-inch squares. The corners of each square must be 90 degrees.

Step 3.
Draw in only one square at a time.
Copy the shapes from the book.
Use the sides and corners of each
square as a guide.

book   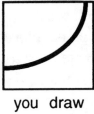   you draw

Step 4.
Continue one square at a time until entire drawing is
complete.

Step 5.

Use scissors to cut out the pattern so you can make the project or a template. Trace around the pattern on the recommended types of material. Use a saber saw to cut out the project or the Masonite template.

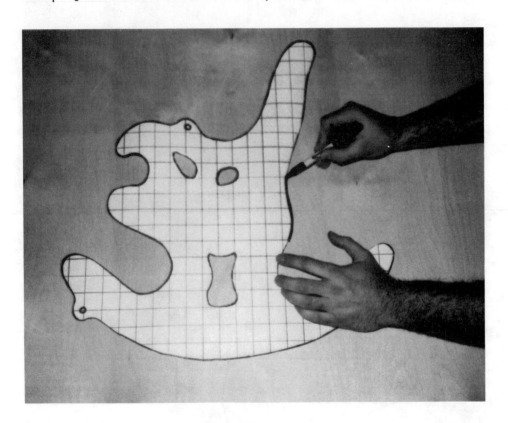

Making a Styrofoam Model

You can use ¾-inch styrofoam to make a model of the projects offered in this book or to create original shapes for projects. Here I am making a styrofoam model of the floor lamp project.

Step 1.
Trace around the template or pattern with a felt marker on the styrofoam.

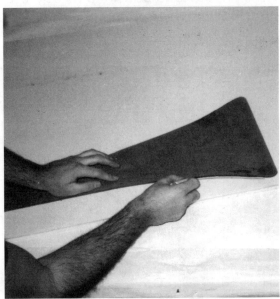

Step 2.
Cut out the styrofoam sections with a saber saw.

Step 3.
Hold the various sections of styrofoam together with toothpicks or small amounts of epoxy, then shape with a right-angle grinder.

Step 4.
Take the model apart and use the various styrofoam sections as a guide to determine the actual size and shape of each plywood lamination of the project.

Cutting Using a Template

When cutting with the router, you will use a ¼-inch-thick Masonite template of the exact shape of the project. With the aid of an inexpensive template guide, the router follows the edge of the Masonite template to cut out the various sections. Masonite tempered on one side, which most lumberyards stock in 4-x-8-foot sheets, is the material I recommend for templates. Your router base will slide easily, and this material is easily repaired with epoxy if you accidentally damage the surfaces with the router cutter.

The rocker and floor lamp templates are "stepped" so the laminations are cut at successively smaller sizes to expedite the shaping process.

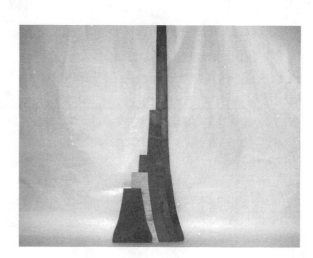

Masonite is easy to cut with a saber saw, and the edges smooth down nicely with a woodworking file. The template is held in place on the wood by a method I developed to speed up production. This method is described in the step-by-step procedure for making the child's rocker in chapter 3.

Laminating

For some projects, laminating is required after the wood has been cut. Five ⅝-inch-thick sections are glued together to make one of the side sections for the adult rocker. This massive characteristic of my designs suggest to many people that the furniture is shaped from large tree trunks. Before the side sections of the rocker are laminated, however, they look like they were cut with a giant cookie cutter—all identical in size and shape.

Laminating is a simple matter of spreading glue on each section, stacking them on top of each other, and clamping them together. Woodworking clamps, handmade clamps, or weights are all methods that I have with good results for squeezing the sections together.

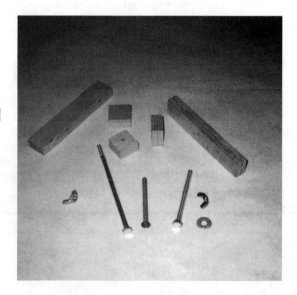

These handmade clamps are made from scrap pieces of Finland birch plywood, wing nuts, washers, and ¼ bolts. Use a twist drill to make holes in the spacers and the end pieces.

If you are laminating three pieces of ⅝-inch plywood together, use three ⅝-inch spacers with the clamps.

Use wing nuts or hex nuts to apply the pressure. Use washers so the nuts will turn easily. Tighten the nuts with pliers or a ratcheting box end wrench.

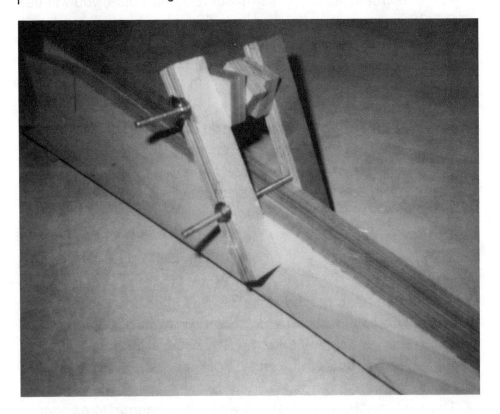

After letting the glue dry overnight, you are ready for the next major stage, shaping.

Shaping

The sculpting or "shaping" is accomplished primarily with two types of tools, the right-angle grinder and the die grinder. For the initial rough grinding, to remove a lot of wood fast, the best grinder to use is a 15-amp right-angle grinder with a 7-inch rubber backing pad, and a 24- or 16-grit hard-backed sanding disk. These are the same type of disks used in auto body work. The 90-degree edges are beveled down and the surfaces are tapered, getting smaller to the outside edges of the project and leaving the middle areas as thick as possible.

For shaping around the tight curves and holes, you will use a 10,000 rpm grinder with a 4½-inch rubber backing pad and 5-inch hard-backed sanding disks. You will also use 16-grit disks with this grinder, too, but for further smoothing, use a 100-grit disk.

For those hard-to-get-at areas, you'll want to use a die grinder with high-speed rotary rasps and rotary files with ¼-inch shanks.

After shaping with these three tools until there are no flat spots and the "grain" patterns flow in a natural way, the project is near completion. Sanding and finishing are the only processes remaining.

Sanding

I use many sanding methods to expedite the smoothing process. Sanding is done using a combination of tools: orbital sander; sanding drums; homemade, pneumatic, and soft disc pads connected to a drill; random orbit sanders; and by hand.

The best method is to start with the pneumatic sander connected to a 2,500 rpm hand drill used to sand the edges and as much of the surfaces as possible. Next, use the random orbit and soft disc pad to sand the remaining surface areas with a fine- grit stick-on disk. Then use sanding drums to smooth the inside of the holes and tight curves. The final sanding step is by hand with 80- and then 100-grit paper.

Finishing

If you plan to stain your project to change the natural color of the wood, now is the time. Remove all sawdust from the previous step before applying the stain. After letting the stain dry overnight, the project is ready for assembly.

Assembly for the rocker means gluing the seat, backrest, and side sections together. I use rope to hold the sections together while the glue is drying. For tables, the legs must be connected to the top with dowel screws.

After assembly, a protective layer of oil finish is applied (tung oil provides the best results). The oil penetrates deep into the pours of the wood and then dries very hard. Apply five or six coats, one coat per day, letting each coat dry overnight. Apply the oil finish with a foam brush, and then rub it into the wood by hand until it is tacky. Use extra-fine steel wool or a finishing pad to smooth after each coat has dried overnight.

After the last coat of finish is dry, lamps can be wired, hinges can be attached to the magic book or the small box, and you can begin to enjoy your completed project.

Outdoor Projects

If you intend to leave the completed project outside at night or in rain, you must use a different method of gluing and finishing. The plywood for the furniture projects must have a waterproof glue between the plies. Marine-grade plywood is one example. The glue used to laminate and assemble the sections of the project together must also be waterproof.

The waterproof finish I recommend is a water-based exterior polyurethane. This type of polyurethane is easy to use. It is nontoxic, dries very fast, and can be cleaned with water. Apply at least five thin coats with a foam brush, sanding lightly with 200-grit sandpaper between coats after the finish is completely dry. Polyurethane is available in high gloss or satin finish. The project will have a professional appearance if you use the satin finish.

Before You Begin

As a follow up to this overview, be sure to read all the safety tips in chapter 2 and review chapter 3, which includes step-by-step instructions (and photos) on building the child's rocker. Do not rush any step of production.

One final note: Be sure to work patiently on every step without skipping any operations. Mistakes caused by rushing will only add to the production time in the long run.

CHAPTER TWO

Safety

This chapter lists the safety rules that relate to the type of woodworking explained in this book. While it is not necessary to memorize every rule listed, try to use the following as a checklist to make your work area safe, and as a guide to help you eliminate personal injury.

Basic woodworking safety practices—such as wearing safety glasses, keeping hands away from moving blades and out of the line of cut, etc.—are things I constantly run through my mind while using the power tools. Woodworking is a lot of fun, and watching a saw blade rapidly cut through a piece of wood is fascinating. But don't let the excitement of the craft distract you to the point that you forget about the moving blade, or where your hands are resting.

General Woodworking Safety Rules

- Wear safety glasses.
- Wear hearing protection when using loud equipment.
- Wear a face mask when using the grinders.
- Always unplug tools and lamps before making any repairs and when changing blades, cutters, sandpaper, or sanding discs.

- Supervise children while they are using power tools.
- Do not talk or look away from work while operating tools.
- Do not force or lean on tools. The motor will burn out, and the tool could cause injury if you slip.
- Cut material only as fast as the machine will cut it easily.
- Make sure the electrical outlets you use are grounded and that you use a GFCI device.
- Wear a respirator during the sanding and grinding operations.
- Never stand on a wet floor when operating a power tool, and never touch faucets or water pipes while holding an electric tool.
- Install smoke detectors in the work area and house.
- If small children have access to the work area, install safety plugs in all outlets.
- Never run an extension cord under a rug. It can become worn and cause a fire.
- Make sure all electric supplies and equipment are approved by Underwriters Laboratories, Inc., an independent, nonprofit testing firm. If the product is approved, the letters "UL" within a circle will appear on the equipment.
- Do not wear loose clothing, chains, or a necktie since these could easily get caught in machinery. Be sure that string from aprons and long hair is tied back.
- Do not use dull blades or cutters.
- Unplug tools when you leave the room.
- Do not leave oily rags and other combustible material in the work area or house. In addition, keep cans of finish and thinners closed and away from flame or sparks.

- Have emergency numbers handy.
- Have a first aid kit available.
- Use oil stain, finishes, and thinners in a well-ventilated room or outside.
- Read and follow the manufacturers' warnings, the maintenance schedules, and the safety rules for each tool used.
- Keep work area clean.
- Have all wiring inspected by an electrician or other qualified person, and never allow children to wire lamps.
- Use double-insulated power tools that have been checked for safety hazards by a certified person.

Using the Band Saw

- Adjust upper guide assembly so it is ¼ inch above work.
- Do not put hands in line with the cut being made. Hold wood to the right or left of blade, not in front of the blade.
- Do not try to remove small pieces of wood from around blade when the machine is running.
- A clicking noise indicates a crack in the blade. Turn the machine off and inspect the blade. If the blade breaks while making a cut, shut off the power and move away from machine until both wheels stop.

Using the Saber Saw

- Place the base of the saw firmly on the wood before starting the cut.
- Turn on the motor before the blade contacts the work.
- Do not hold wood with your hands or put your hand in line with the cut being made.

- Use a blade $\frac{3}{16}$ inch or less when cutting sharp curves.

Using the Router

- Securely mount the cutter shaft to a depth of at least $\frac{1}{2}$ inch, and tighten the base securely.
- Keep the router cutter clear of wood before turning on motor.
- When the cut is complete, turn off the motor and do not lift the machine from the work until the motor has stopped.

CHAPTER THREE

Building the child's rocker

Assuming you have read chapters 1 and 2 carefully, you are ready to try your first project. This chapter includes step-by-step photos that were taken in sequence as I constructed a child's rocker, but you will use the same procedures for making the rest of the furniture projects in this book. The smaller projects, which require no lamination, will still utilize the shaping procedures shown here.

I suggest you read this chapter thoroughly before beginning any project, as its instructions are the most in-depth and you might want to refer back to it as you construct other pieces.

CHILD'S ROCKER

Supplies

1   sheet 4'-x-5'-x-¾"(or ⅝") Finland birch plywood
2   quarts woodworking glue
2   16- or 24-grit hard-backed sanding discs
1   80- or 100-grit hard-backed sanding discs
3   pkgs. of ½", ¼", 1" sanding drum sleeves
1   3" sanding sleeve, 80- or 100-grit
2   fine or medium grit sticks on sanding discs for random
     orbit or pad sanders
2   pkgs. of 80-, 150-, 200-grit sandpaper

1   quart oil stain
1   pint tung oil finish
1   fine steel wool or finishing pad
1   quart of mineral spirits (for cleaning)
2   2" foam brushes
2   pkgs. sanding sleeves for dremel tool sanding drums

Tools (* indicates optional tools for faster production)
4½" or 5" right-angle mini grinder
saber saw with ³⁄₁₆" blade
hand drill with ⅜" chuck
router with template guide & ¼" straight cutter
clamps
rotary rasps
½", ¾", 1" sanding drums
standard ⅜" twist drill
soft 5" sanding pad
orbital sander
heavy-duty staple gun & staples
hammer
screwdriver
wood file
safety glasses
respirator
scissors
*Dremel tool with sanding drums & rotary files
*portable band saw
*random orbit sander with soft backing pad
*3" pneumatic sander with 2500 rpm hand drill
*7" right-angle grinder with flexible backing pad
*die grinder with rotary file

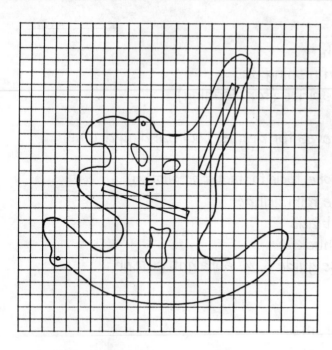

Cut 6 sections of piece E, 2 with mortises.

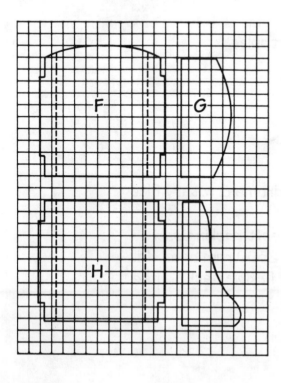

Dotted line shows size & location of lamination for back rest (F) & bottom of seat (H). Number of sections needed: F-2 (1 without tenons); G-2; H-2 (1 without tenons): I-2.

Step 1. Enlarge the pattern.

The paper pattern is all you need if you will be using a saber saw for the cutting process. You can see the one-inch squares I drew on the pattern for enlarging the rocker shape. (See chapter 1 for instructions on enlarging the patterns provided in the book.) Use the Masonite template if you are using a router for the cutting process. The square-shaped template and small curved template are used for making the seat and backrest sections. The small tongue shapes sticking out from the edge of the rocker's side section are used for holding the template on the wood.

Step 2. Drill holes for the dowels.

Here the Masonite template is secured to the birch plywood in preparation for cutting with a router. (If you are cutting with a saber saw, merely trace around the edge of the paper template with a pencil and cut with a medium-toothed blade.)

The electric hand drill in this picture is fitted with a drill guide attachment. This helpful device takes the guesswork out of making a 90-degree hole to a flat surface, and a depth stop keeps the drill from marring the workbench.

Use a $\frac{3}{8}$-inch twist drill to drill the holes. The hole in the template tongues shows you exactly where to drill. Drill one hole all the way through the plywood. Next tap in a $\frac{3}{8}$-inch hardwood dowel until it is all the way down and flat with the top of the template.

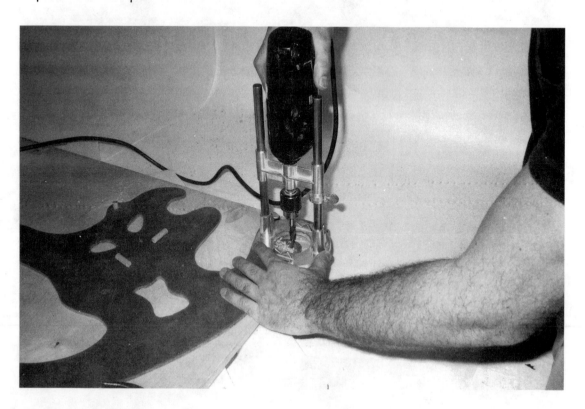

Repeat this pegging process with the rest of the holes. Remember to drill and peg one hole at a time. If you drill all the holes without doweling, the template could slip and the holes will not align. Notice that the template is as close as possible to the edge to conserve wood. The styrofoam under the plywood keeps the router cutter from cutting into the work table. Styrofoam can also be used when using a saber saw for cutting.

Step 3. Cut around the template.
Push the router around the template in a counterclockwise direction using a ¼-inch carbide-tipped straight cutter and a template guide attached to your router. The template guide slides against the edge of the Masonite to reproduce an exact copy of the template shape. Do not try to cut all the

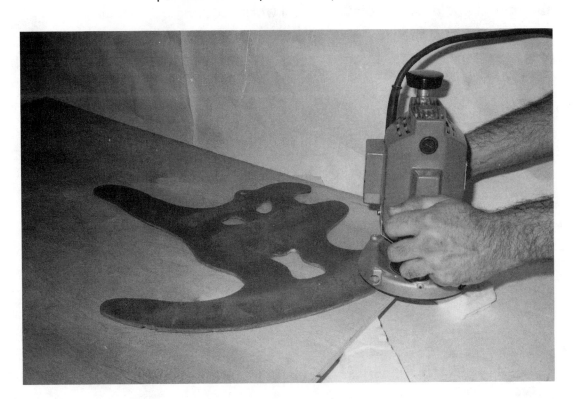

way through the entire ⅝-inch sheet of plywood with one
pass. Go all the way around at a depth of only ⅛-inch, then
drop the cutter 3⁄16 inch, and go all the way around again.
Repeat until the cutter goes all the way through the wood.

   The router pictured adjusts easily to three preset depths
with a handy depth-stop feature. Keep the router base flat
against the Masonite template.

Step 4. Remove the dowels.
Here, the first side section is completely cut. Use the center
punch to remove the hardwood dowels. A large common nail
hammered upside-down on the dowel works, too.

Step 5. Cut the rest of the side sections.

Sweep off the sawdust and secure the template again for another side section. Interlock the template with the previous cut as much as possible to conserve wood. You will need six of these sections for the child's rocker, and ten for the adult rocker.

Step 6. Cut the mortises.

Using the router, cut the mortises
(slot) that will hold the seat and
backrest. I use a separate
template for this cut because
putting a slot in the other
template would weaken it, and
the larger surface area helps keep
the router from tipping. Cut the
mortise to a depth of ½ inch, and
be sure to cut it before cutting
the side section out (this
prevents the wood from moving
too much). Avoid boat patches
around the mortises because they
will show up on the finished
product. Turn the mortising
template over for the second side
so the mortises will face each
other to accept the seat and
backrest.

Step 7.
Cut the seat and backrest.

After tracing the seat and backrest
templates, cut them out with a
saber saw. (I use the router to cut
these sections for the adult rocker.)
Cut one seat section and backrest
section with the tenons and one
each without the tenons. The ones
without the tenons will be glued on
for thickness. (See step 10.)

Step 8.
Prepare the wood for gluing.

Use a woodworking file to remove any splinters around the edges of all the sections. If you don't, they will get mixed in with the glue during the next step. Also at this point, open the dowel holes larger with a $\frac{13}{32}$ inch twist drill.

Step 9. Glue the side sections together.

Using a foam brush, spread an even layer of woodworking glue on the surfaces that will come in contact with each other. Use $\frac{3}{8}$-inch hardwood dowels to keep the three sections lined up during this step. Use the same pegging holes that were used to hold the template for cutting.

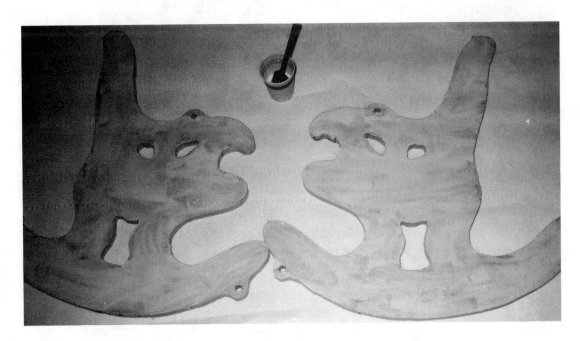

Step 10. Clamp the laminations.

Here woodworking clamps are used to apply even pressure all the way around the sections. A slight amount of glue squeezed out all the way around indicates proper clamping and an adequate amount of glue.

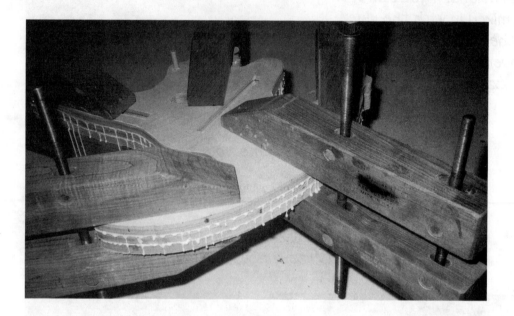

Step 11. Glue the seat and backrest sections.

Here the seat and backrest are being clamped. It is very important to line up the small pieces for the seat and backrest with the tenons. If they slip while glue is setting up, there will be a gap where the tenon fits into the mortises. The larger piece without the tenon (on the bottom) does not have to be lined up and can even stick out on the front and back. This piece is ground down flush during the shaping process. Fasten heavy-duty staples to edges to keep pieces from slipping while the glue dries. After the glue dries, use a woodworking chisel to remove the excess glue around the tenons. The glue will cut off easily if it is not allowed to dry for more than an hour.

Step 12. Do initial rough shaping.

After using the 15-amp and 10,000 rpm grinders for rough shaping, I check the taper and contours. A handscrew clamp is used to hold the work while grinding. Use the dark glue lines as a guide when determining the amount of wood to remove.

Notice that about ⅝ inch of the edge is left flat all the way around. A 16- or 23-grit hard-backed sanding disk is used with both grinders, and the alignment tongues are ground down with these tools.

Step 13. Grind the inside of the side section.

On the inside of the side sections, grind only three plies deep, staying away from the mortises. The mortise area where the seat and backrest interlock with the side sections is perfectly flat. If you grind in too far from the edge, you will have a gap between the sections.

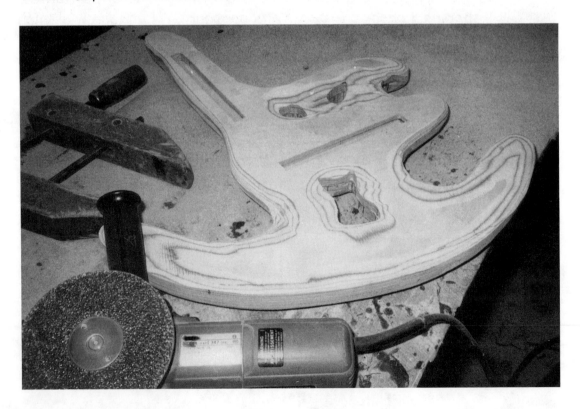

Step 14. Shape the holes and tight curves.

A die grinder with a rotary file is used to shape around the holes and tight curves. This type of spiral cutter removes wood fast and leaves a surface smooth enough to sand with the sanding drums. Notice how the handscrew clamp is used to hold the side section upright. Move the sections around often to accommodate a comfortable operating position when using the power tools.

Step 15.
Sand the side sections smooth.
Use a small grinder with a 100-grit hard-backed disk to sand the wood smooth. Be sure to take the time at this step to create "grain" lines that curve and flow in a natural pattern. If you notice a straight glue line, more sanding is required in that area.

Step 16. Sand the tight areas.
Use a drum sander with a medium-grit sanding sleeve for the tight areas. Further sanding is done with the pneumatic sander using first an 80-grit sanding sleeve then a 100-grit

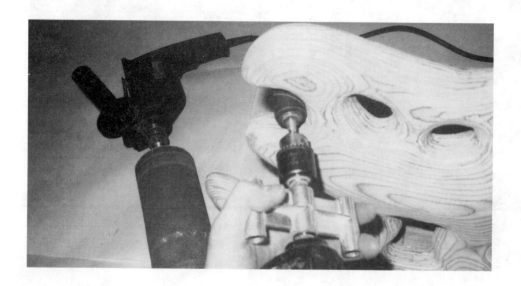

sleeve. Remember to use the pneumatic sander with a 2,500 rpm hand drill. A slower drill is better for sanding with the sanding drums.

Step 17. Sand the seat and backrest.

Because sanding drums and the pneumatic sander will not work on the concave sections of the seat and backrest, I use a soft disc pad and a medium-grit stick on sanding disk with a hand drill. Check all parts of the rocker closely, and use this tool to sand any areas you are unable to reach with the other sanders. A random orbit sander works well for these areas also.

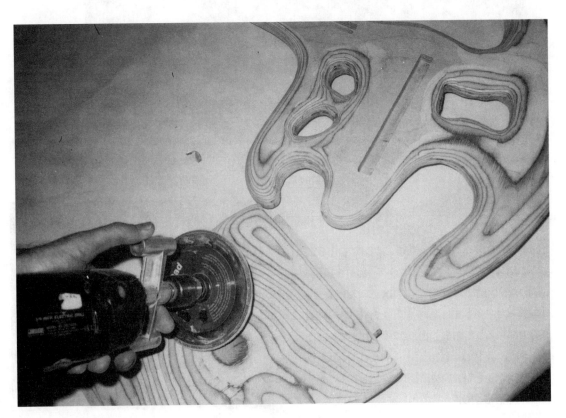

Step 18. Hand-sand the project.

Using an old 100-grit sanding sleeve (from the pneumatic sander) like a glove, sand the entire project by hand.

Step 19. Apply the stain.

Use a foam brush to apply oil stain if you want to change the natural color of the birch. I mix 3 parts light oak stain with 1 part walnut stain. Let this dry overnight. The color will look dull the next day, but the next step will bring out the desired color.

Step 20. Apply glue to the mortises and tenons.
Using a foam brush, spread white or yellow water-based woodworker's glue in the mortises and around the tenons. Do not over-glue, or it will drip on the project.

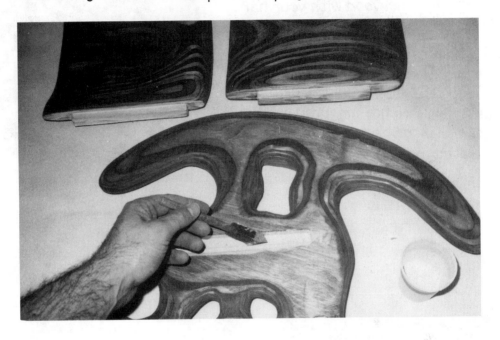

Step 21.
Secure sections with cord.
Use rope or heavy cord to hold sections together while glue is drying. Use a damp cloth to wipe off any excess glue that squeezes from the joints. Let dry overnight if glue is wiped with a damp cloth.

Step 22. Apply tung oil.

With a foam brush, spread a thin coat of satin tung oil over the entire rocker. Rub the oil into the pores of the wood with your hands. Let dry overnight. Waterless soap lotion is good for cleaning hands after this step. Use the tung oil sparingly. If you put the oil on too heavy it will not dry properly. Work it well into the pores of the wood, leaving no drips or runs.

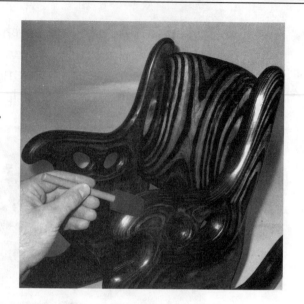

Step 23. Smooth the finish.

The next day, use a fine finishing pad to smooth the oil finish. Extra-fine steel wool works well, too, but it is harder to dust off. Repeat steps 22 and 23 for at least three coats. More coats will provide more protection for the wood and increase the gloss. Do not use steel wool after the final coat. Project is now finished. Deliver to the quality control inspector.

Adult Rocker

To make the adult-sized rocker, you will need more materials and supplies, but the instructions are the same. Use the larger pattern provided and the following tools & materials list to construct the adult rocker.

ADULT ROCKER

Supplies

6 sheets 4'-x-5'-x-¾" Finland birch plywood
1 gallon woodworking glue
5 16- or 24-grit hard-backed sanding discs
3 80- or 100-grit hard-backed sanding discs

10 pkgs. of ½", ¼", 1" sanding drum sleeves
2   3" sanding sleeves, 80- or 100-grit
2   fine or medium grit sticks on sanding discs for random
    orbit or pad sanders
5   pkgs. of 80-, 150-, 200-grit sandpaper
2   quarts oil stain
1   quart tung oil finish
1   fine steel wool or finishing pad
1   quart of mineral spirits (for cleaning)
2   2" foam brushes
2   pkgs. sanding sleeves for dremel tool sanding drums

Tools (* indicates optional tools for faster production)
4½" or 5" right-angle mini grinder
saber saw with ³⁄₁₆" blade
hand drill with ⅜" chuck
router with template guide & ¼" straight cutter
clamps
rotary rasps
½", ¾", 1" sanding drums
standard ³⁄₈" twist drill
soft 5" sanding pad
orbital sander
heavy-duty staple gun & staples
hammer
screwdriver
wood file
safety glasses
respirator
scissors
*Dremel tool with sanding drums and rotary files

*portable band saw
*random orbit sander with soft backing pad
*3" pneumatic sander with 2500 rpm hand drill
*7" right-angle grinder with flexible backing pad
*die grinder with rotary file

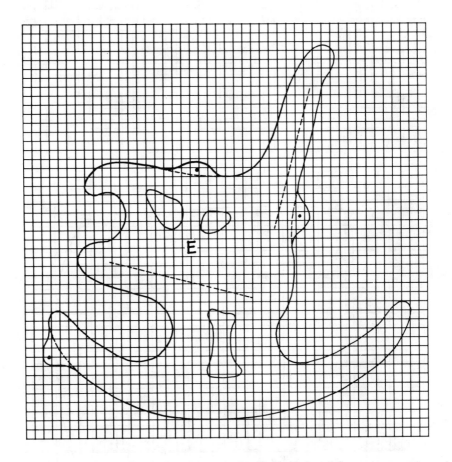

Cut 10 of section E, mortises on 2 only. (one square = 1" x 1".) Dotted lines show size & location for backrest and bottom of seat and center line for mortise

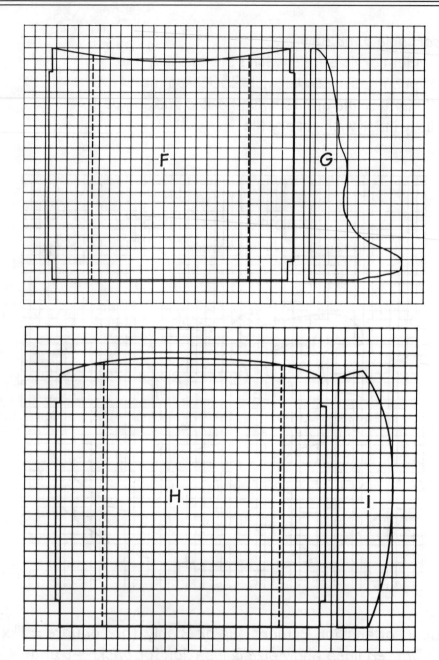

Dotted lines indicate where alignment tongues are cut off.
One square = 1" x 1". Number of sections needed: F-2 (1
without tenons); G-2; H-2 (1 without tenons); I-2.

CHAPTER FOUR

Model sailboat

While this toy sailboat is not designed to float on water, it is a great decoration idea for a desk or dresser. Use two different colors of wood for contrast between the sail and hull. (I used butternut for the hull and pine for the sail.)

MODEL SAILBOAT

Supplies

1   1'-x-2'-x-1" stock in pine, cherry, butternut, walnut, etc.
1   ¼"-x-2" wooden dowel or metal rod
1   8 oz. bottle woodworking glue
1   16- or 24-grit hard-backed sanding disc
1   80- or 100-grit hard-backed sanding disc
1   pkg. of ½", ¼", 1" sanding drum sleeves
1   3" sanding sleeve, 80- or 100-grit
1   fine- or medium-grit sticks on sanding discs for random
    orbit or pad sanders
2   pkgs. of 80-, 150-, 200-grit sandpaper
1   ½ pint oil stain
1   ½ pint tung oil finish
1   extra-fine steel wool or finishing pad
1   quart of mineral spirits (for cleaning)
2   2" foam brushes

Tools (* indicates optional tools for faster production)

coping saw
hand drill with ⅜" chuck
orbital sander
rasp
wood file
safety glasses
respirator
scissors
1/16", ⅛", ¼" twist drill
*4½" or 5" right-angle mini grinder
*saber saw with 3/16" blade
*3" pneumatic sander with 2500 rpm hand drill
*random orbit sander with soft backing pad
*portable band saw

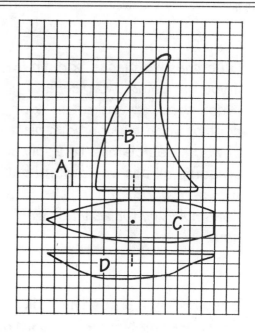

Dotted line shows location of mast (A). One square = 1" x 1". Number of sections needed: A-1; B-1; C (top view of hull)-1; D (side vew of hull)-1.

Step 1. Trace the hull pattern.

Trace the hull pattern on 1-inch or 2-inch-thick wood. Use a handsaw or saber saw to cut the wood to approximate length and width. You will need two pieces for the hull if you are using 1-inch wood. If you are using 2-inch wood, you will need only one piece of wood, so you can skip the next step.

Step 2.
Glue the two pieces together.

If you are using two pieces of 1-inch wood, spread a thin even coat of wood glue on both pieces of wood. Use clamps to apply even pressure all the way around both pieces of wood, and let the assembly dry for at least one hour.

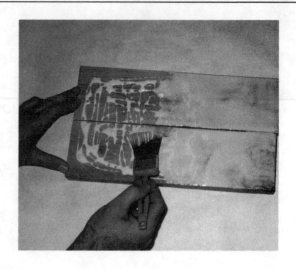

Step 3. Trace & cut the sail.

After tracing the sail pattern onto a 1¼-inch piece of wood (I used pine), use a portable band saw, saber saw, or coping saw to cut out the sail and hull.

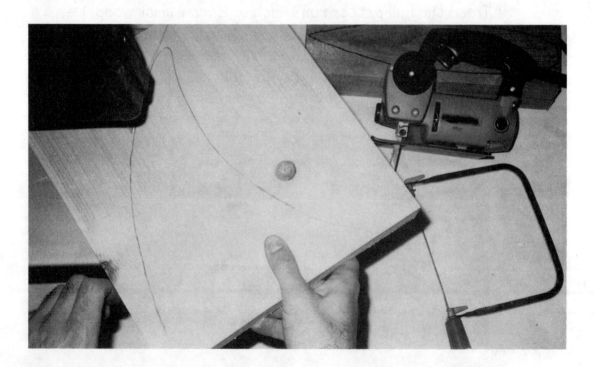

Step 4. Shape the sail.
Here, Kevin uses a die grinder to shape the sail. Use a clamp to secure work to table. You can also use a Dremel tool to taper the sail. A high-speed right-angle grinder works the fastest. Use a 24-grit sanding disc first, then an 80-grit disc for smoothing.

Step 5. Sand both pieces.
Clamp pneumatic sander and drill to table for sanding or sand by hand. Use 80-grit sandpaper first, then 100-grit.

Step 6. Cut the mast.
Use a coping saw to cut mast from a ¼-inch hardwood dowel.

Step 7.
Prepare the project for assembly.
Make a trial assembly, then use a ¼-inch twist drill and hand drill to drill a 1-inch-deep hole in the sail and hull. Next, make a final sanding by hand with 220-grit sandpaper, sanding along the grain, not across it.

Step 8. Apply tung oil finish.
Brush on a thin coat of tung oil
over the sail and hull. Let it dry
overnight. Use extra-fine steel
wool to smooth the finish, then
brush on another coat of tung oil
and let it dry overnight. Repeat
this finishing process until the
desired gloss is achieved, then
assemble the project.

CHAPTER FIVE

Boomerang

Boomerangs are easy to make, but throwing them so they will return takes practice. This basic design is very accurate, but be sure to practice throwing it in a field away from cars, houses, and people.

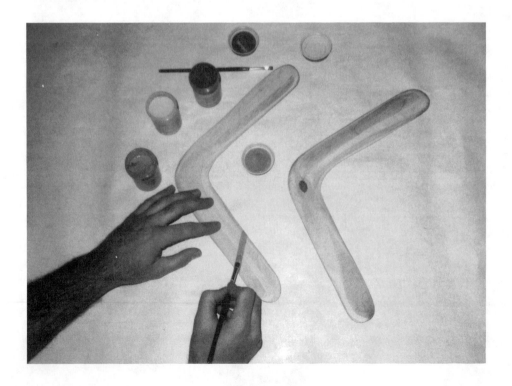

BOOMERANG

Supplies

¼ sheet 4'-x-5'-x-¼" Finland birch plywood
1   16- or 24-grit hard-backed sanding disc
1   80- or 100-grit hard-backed sanding disc
1   pkg. ½", ¼", 1" sanding drum sleeves
1   3" sanding sleeve, 80- or 100-grit
1   fine- or medium-grit sticks on sanding discs for random
     orbit or pad sanders
1   pkg. of 80-, 150-, 200-grit sandpaper
2   2" foam brushes
½ pint oil stain
½ pint tung oil finish or paint
1   extra-fine steel wool or finishing pad
1   quart of mineral spirits

Tools (* indicates optional tools for faster production)
4½" or 5" right-angle mini grinder with flexible backing pad
wood file
coping saw
orbital sander
safety glasses
respirator
scissors
*saber saw with ³⁄₁₆" wide blade
*pneumatic sander with 2500 rpm hand drill
*random orbit sander with soft backing pad
*portable band saw

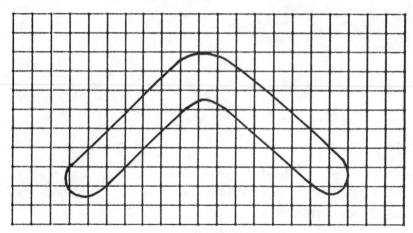

One square = 1" x 1". One section needed.

Step 1. Trace the pattern.
Trace the pattern onto ¼-inch-thick Finland or Baltic birch plywood.

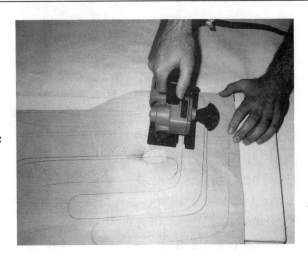

Step 2. Cut out the project.

Use a band saw or a saber saw to cut out the project. Place the wood on 2-inch styrofoam when using a saber saw.

Step 3. Begin grinding.

Clamp the work securely, then taper the bottom of boomerang with a mini grinder equipped with a 24-grit disc. The black mark on the project shows the amount of wood to be removed across entire bottom.

Step 4. Make the undercut.

Now that bottom is tapered, hollow a slight undercut where you see the "XXX" marks. This slight hollow will be against the palm of your hand when throwing. The *airfoil* (top) and the *undercut* (bottom) are reversed for left- and right-handed people. If you are left-handed and make the right-handed boomerang you will not be able to throw it, and vice versa.

Step 5. Make the airfoil.

The top of the boomerang is the same shape as an airplane wing. This airfoil is shaped with the right-angle grinder also. Righties will spin through the air counterclockwise; lefties will spin clockwise. The edge leading into the air is thick but rounded slightly. Taper wood down to the trailing edge to about ⅛ inch.

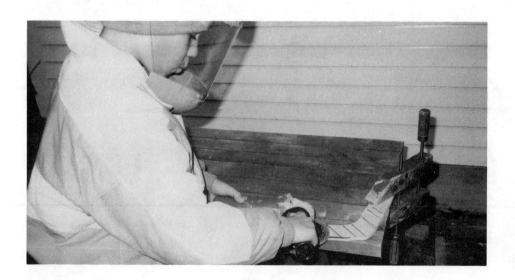

Step 6.
Sand & finish the project.
Use a pneumatic sander (pictured here) to smooth, or sand by hand with 80-grit then 100-grit sandpaper. An orbital sander or random orbit sander works well also. Make a final sanding by hand with 220-grit sandpaper, and paint the boomerang with bright-colored enamel paint.

Step 7. Determine wind direction.
A piece of cloth or paper can be attached to a post to help determine the wind direction. Kevin is left-handed, so he throws into the wind at a slight angle. Right-handed people would throw to the right of the post at same angle. If the wind is blowing hard, hold the boomerang almost straight up.

Step 8. Release the boomerang.
Snap your wrist hard when
releasing so the boomerang spins
fast. If the boomerang goes over
your head when it returns, throw it
lower to the ground next time and
hold it up straighter when
releasing it.

CHAPTER SIX

Magic book

Amagic book can be used for binding things like treasure maps, secret messages, classic children's stories, plastic photo sleeves, or just plain paper for drawing or coloring. Birch plywood or any of your favorite types of wood is suitable for this unique project.

MAGIC BOOK

Supplies

1'-x-3'-x-1" stock in pine, cherry, butternut, walnut, etc.
1   16- or 24-grit hard-backed sanding discs
1   80- or 100-grit hard-backed sanding discs
2   pkgs. ½", ¼", 1" sanding drum sleeves
1   3" sanding sleeve for pneumatic sander, 80- or 100-grit
1   fine- or medium-grit stick on sanding disc for random
     orbit or pad sanders
2   pkgs. 80-, 150-, 200-grit sandpaper
2   2" foam brushes
½   pint oil stain
½   pint tung oil finish
1   extra-fine steel wool or finishing pad
1   quart mineral spirits
2   decorative metal hinges with screws
3   accounting book pins with posts, at least 1½" long
1¾" wooden knob

Tools (* indicates optional tools for faster production)
hand drill with ⅜" chuck
clamps
½", ¾", 1" sanding drums
screwdriver
wood file
rasp
coping saw
orbital sander
safety glasses
respirator
scissors
⅙", ⅛", ¼" twist drill

*portable band saw
*surform tool
*random orbit sander with soft backing pad
*pneumatic sander with 2500 rpm hand drill
*4½" or 5" right-angle mini grinder with flexible backing pad
*saber saw with ³⁄₁₆" blade

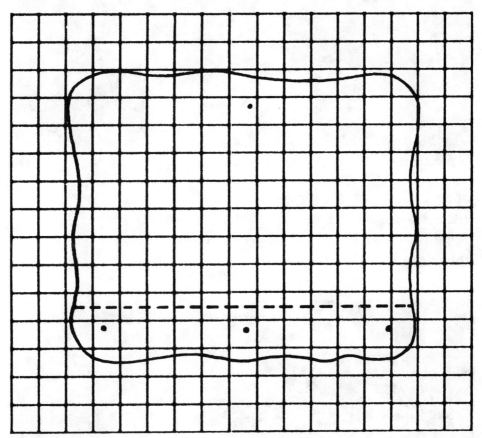

One square = 1" x 1". Two sections of cover needed. Dotted line shows where front cover is cut & hinged.

Step 1. Trace the pattern.

Trace the pattern twice on wood at least 1-inch thick. For this sequence I use 1¼-inch pine. The dotted lines show where the front cover will bend. The holes on the pattern show the location of binding pins and handle.

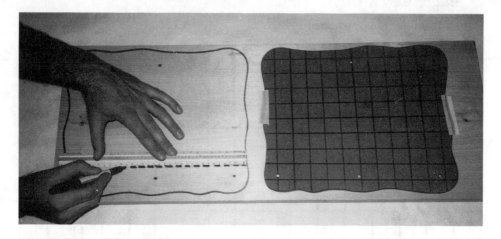

Step 2. Cut out the project.

Use a band saw or a saber saw to cut out the project. Remember to use 2-inch styrofoam under wood when using saber saw.

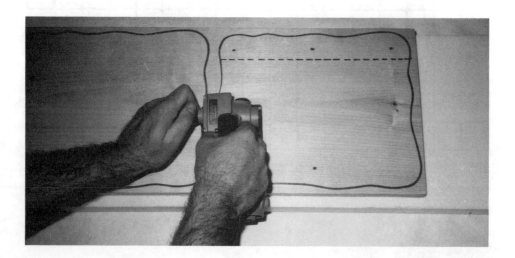

Step 3. Taper the outside.
Use a right-angle grinder with a 24-grit sanding disc to taper the outside of the covers, leaving the middle section as thick as possible. Taper to $\frac{3}{8}$ inch around the edge, and smooth with a 100-grit disc.

Step 4. Smooth the surfaces.
Use an orbital sander or a random orbit sander to smooth surfaces. The sanding discs shown stick on the pads with adhesive for quick changing. The inside of the covers stay flat.

Step 5. Drill holes for handle and binding pins.

On the front cover, drill the holes for the handle and binding pins. The drill and pins I use are ⅛ inch in diameter, and the accounting bookbinding pins like the ones I used can be purchased at an office supply store. Do not drill the back cover yet.

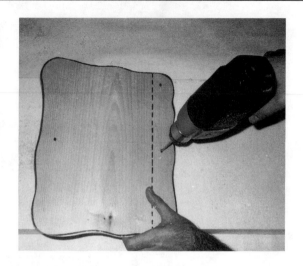

Step 6. Drill through both covers.

Clamp the two covers together in position. Drill through the three holes (for the binding pins) you made in Step 5 all the way through the back cover. All three holes will be aligned perfectly. NOTE: Do not drill the handle hole into the back cover.

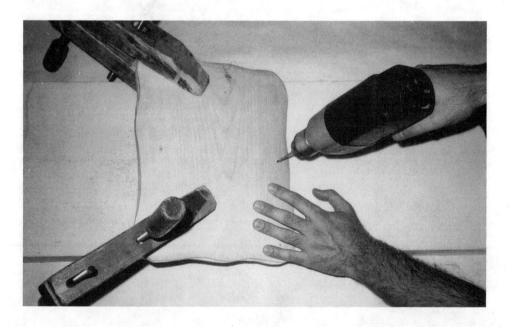

Step 7. Shape the covers.
While the covers are still clamped, use a drum sander and an electric drill to sand around edges. This will make both covers the same shape and size.

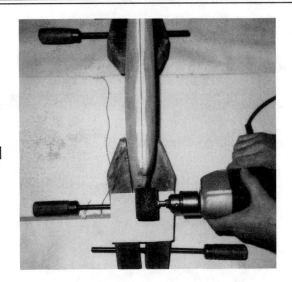

Step 8. Make the cut in the front cover.
Using a saber saw, cut along the dotted line where front cover will bend. An extra piece of 2-inch styrofoam is helpful in keeping the wood from rocking during this operation. Use an orbital sander to smooth the edge after cutting, then sand by hand with 220-grit sandpaper.

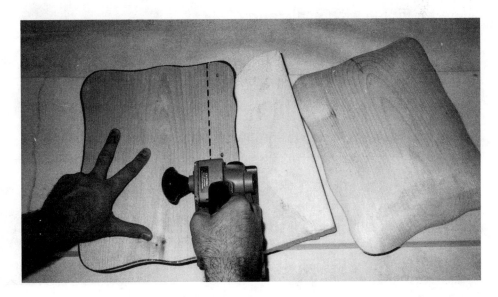

Step 9. Illustrate the cover.

Use graphite transfer paper to transfer a picture, or draw your own picture lightly with a pencil on the inside of the covers. Then use a wood burner to etch in a brown burn line over the drawing. Do not use a wax-based transfer paper. The wax will melt into the pores of the wood.

Step 10. Finish with stain and oil.

If you like, you can now change the color of the wood with oil stain and let it dry overnight. Then, over the natural wood or stained surface, brush a thin coat of tung oil over both sides, and let this dry overnight. The next day, lightly smooth the project with extra-fine steel wood, apply another coat of tung oil, and let it dry overnight. Repeat this finishing process until desired gloss is achieved.

Step 11.
Assemble the magic book.
Mark paper and punch holes with a paper punch. Assemble paper or photo sleeves with accounting book pins and a screwdriver.

Step 12. Attach hinges.
Attach hinges with the small wood screws (included in the hinge package) and a screwdriver. Here I am making a pilot hole with a hand drill and twist drill slightly smaller than the screw diameter. Drill one hole, then fasten with a screw before proceeding to ensure that the holes line up with the hinge.

CHAPTER SEVEN

Wall Rack

A wall rack is great for holding keys, gloves, jewelry, and other small items. For this sequence, I used ½-inch cup hooks, but you could also use ⅛-inch hardwood dowels (pictured in the project photo) instead of the brass hooks.

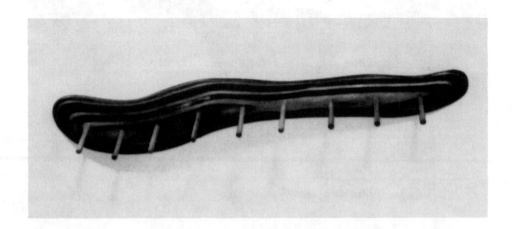

WALL RACK

Supplies

1 4"-x-2"-x-1" stock in pine, cherry, butternut, walnut, etc.
1 3/16"-x-3' hardwood dowel *or* pkg. of 3/8" brass cup hooks
1 16- or 24-grit hard-backed sanding disc
1 80- or 100-grit hard-backed sanding disc
1 pkg. 1/2", 1/4", 1" sanding drum sleeves
1 3" sanding sleeve for pneumatic sander, 80- & 100-grit
1 fine- or medium-grit stick on sanding discs for random orbit or pad sanders
1 pkg. 80-, 150-, 200-grit sandpaper
2 2" foam brushes
1 pint oil stain
1/2 pint tung oil finish
1 extra-fine steel wool or finishing pad
1 quart mineral spirits
9 1/2" brass cup hooks or 1/8" hardwood dowels

Tools (* indicates optional tools for faster production)
1/2", 3/4", 1" sanding drums
wood file
rasp
coping saw
orbital sander
safety glasses
respirator
scissors
1/16", 1/8", 1/4" twist drill
* portable band saw
* surform tool
* Dremel tool with sanding drums & rotary files
* soft 5" sanding pad

*random orbit sander with soft backing pad
*4½" or 5" right-angle mini grinder with flexible backing pad
*saber saw with ³⁄₁₆" blade
*hand drill with ³⁄₈" chuck
*3" pneumatic sander with 2500 rpm hand drill

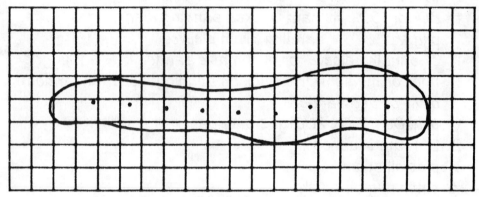

One square = 1" x 1". One section needed.

Step 1. Trace & cut the pattern.
Trace the pattern onto birch plywood or any wood at least
1 inch thick. Megan is using a coping saw here to cut out the
project, but you could also use a band saw or a saber saw.

Step 2. Round the edges.
Clamp the project to a table and use a large rasp or electric grinder to round the edge all the way around. Leave the back flat. A surform tool is also a fun and safe one to use for shaping.

Step 3. Sand the project.
Clamp the pneumatic sander and drill to a table and sand the rack with an 80-grit sanding sleeve, then sand by hand with 220-grit sandpaper. Do not sand across the grain of wood; this will scratch your project.

Step 4. Apply the finish.
Brush a thin coat of tung oil on the project and let it dry overnight. The next day, smooth the rack with steel wool, and repeat this finishing process until desired gloss is achieved.

Step 5. Add hooks or dowels.
Mark the location of the cup hooks, then make a small starter hole with a tiny finishing nail and hammer. Push and turn hooks into the wood clockwise.

CHAPTER EIGHT

Small boxes

There are three fast ways to hollow out these small wooden boxes that can be used to hold anything from jewelry to harmonicas.

SMALL BOXES

Supplies

1   6"-x-2'-x-1" stock (pine, cherry, butternut, walnut, etc.)
1   8 oz. bottle woodworking glue
1   16- or 24-grit hard-backed sanding disc
1   80- or 100-grit hard-backed sanding disc
2   pkgs. ½", ¼", 1" sanding drum sleeves
1   3" sanding sleeve for pneumatic sander, 80- & 100-grit
1   fine- or medium-grit stick on sanding discs for random
     orbit or pad sanders
1   pkg. 80-, 150-, 200-grit sandpaper
2   2" foam brushes
1   pkg. sanding sleeves for dremel tool
½   pint oil stain
½   pint tung oil finish
1   extra-fine steel wool or finishing pad
1   quart mineral spirits
2   decorative hinges with screws
3   accounting book pins with posts at least 1½" long

Tools (*indicates optional tool for faster production)
clamps
rotary rasps
½", ¾", 1" sanding drums
standard ⅜" twist drill
soft 5" sanding pad
screwdriver
wood file
rasp
coping saw
orbital sander
safety glasses

respirator

scissors

* ½" Forstner bit

* Dremel tool with sanding drums & rotary files

* portable band saw

* soft 5" sanding pad

* random orbit sander with soft backing pad

* 4½" or 5" right-angle mini grinder with flexible backing pad

* saber saw with $^3\!/\!_{16}$" blade

* hand drill with $^3\!/\!_8$" chuck

* $^1\!/\!_{16}$", $^1\!/\!_8$", $^1\!/\!_4$" twist drill

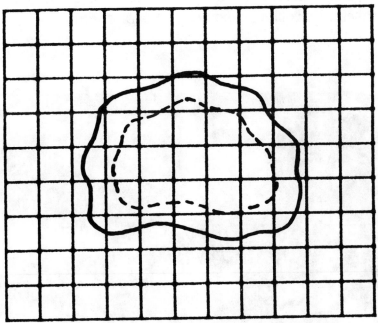

One square = 1" x 1". For each box, 3 box sections, 1 top, and 1 bottom are needed. Dotted line shows where to hollow out inside of box.

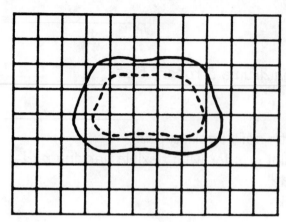

One square = 1" x 1". For each box, 3 box sections, 1 top, and 1 bottom are needed. Dotted line shows where to hollow out inside of box.

Step 1. Trace the pattern.

Trace patterns on wood at least 1 inch thick. The dotted line indicates where the boxes will be hollowed out.

Step 2. Hollow out the boxes.

For one method, drill four ½-inch holes inside the dotted lines at the corners, then use a saber saw to cut around the dotted line.

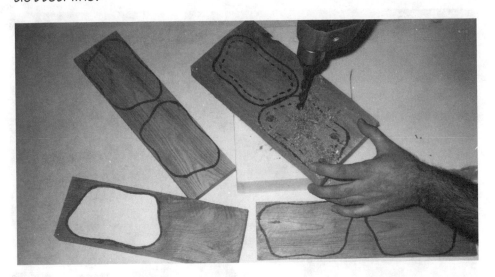

A second method involves using a ½-inch Forstner bit and an electric hand drill. Staying on the inside of the dotted line, drill to the same depth each time. Do not drill all the way through the box.

A third way to hollow the box is by cutting with a band saw. The screwdriver is holding open the point where the band saw blade entered.

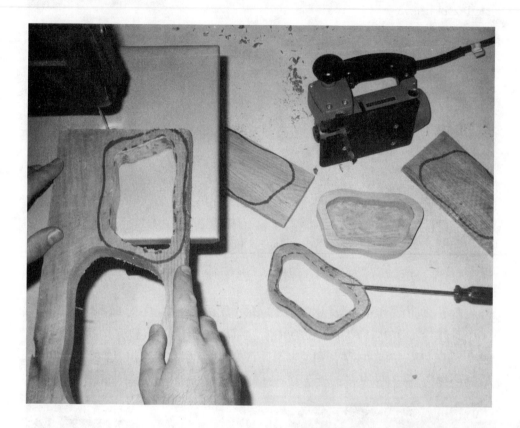

NOTE: If you use the saber saw or band saw method, a piece of wood must be glued on to form the bottom of the box.

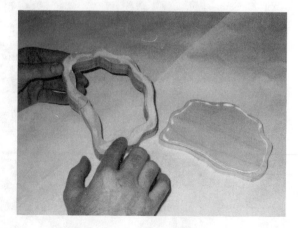

Step 3. Smooth the inside of the box.
Use a die grinder or Dremel tool to smooth inside of box. Use drum sanders and an electric hand drill or Dremel tool for further sanding.

Step 4. Sand the outside.
Clamp the top in position and proceed with rounding over the edges of box. Use a mini grinder with a 24-grit sanding disc for this operation (shown in photo). With the project still clamped, use a pneumatic, orbital, or random orbit sander with 80- grit paper to smooth, then sand by hand with 100-grit sandpaper.

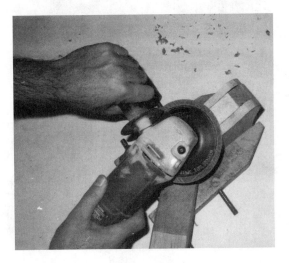

Step 5.
Finish with oil & sanding.

Brush on a thin coat of tung oil and let it dry overnight. Finish all sides of the box. The next day, smooth lightly with extra-fine steel wool, and repeat the finishing process at least two more times.

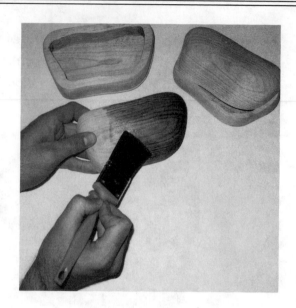

Step 6. Add the hinges.

Use small hinges with wood screws to fasten the top of box. Use a twist drill half the diameter of the screws to drill a pilot hole for screws. Drill one at a time, secure the screw, then proceed to next hole.

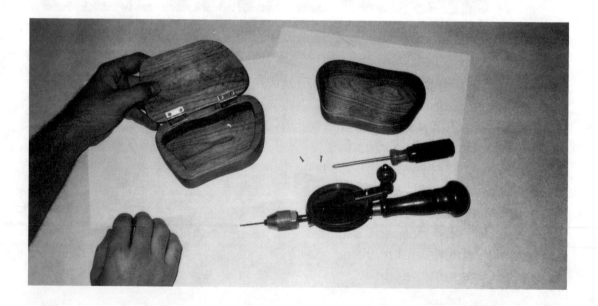

CHAPTER NINE

Miniature furniture

These miniature projects will be a welcome addition to any doll house. The sizes of the chairs and table can easily be altered to accommodate any size doll or to accommodate any size doll house.

MINIATURE FURNITURE

Supplies

1   1'-x-3'-x-1" stock (pine, cherry, butternut, walnut) or ¾" or ⅜" birch plywood
1   8 oz. bottle woodworking glue
1   16- or 24-grit hard-backed sanding disc
1   80- or 100-grit hard-backed sanding disc
1   pkg. ½", ¼", 1" sanding drum sleeves
1   3" sanding sleeve for pneumatic sander, 80- & 100-grit
1   fine- or medium-grit stick on sanding discs for random orbit or pad sanders
1   pkg. 80-, 150-, 200-grit sandpaper
2   2" foam brushes
2   pkgs. sanding sleeves for dremel tool
½   quart oil stain
½   pint tung oil finish
1   quart mineral spirits
1   ¼" & ½" hardwood dowels
1   3'-x-1' piece of fabric

Tools (*indicates optional tool for faster production)
hand drill with ⅜" chuck
½", ¾", 1" sanding drums
wood file
rasp
coping saw
orbital sander
safety glasses
respirator
scissors
1/16", ⅛", ¼" twist drill
*4½" or 5" right-angle mini grinder with flexible backing pad

* die grinder with rotary file
* saber saw with $\frac{3}{16}$" blade
* rotary rasps
* random orbit sander with soft backing pad
* surform tool
* Dremel tool with sanding drums & rotary files
* portable band saw

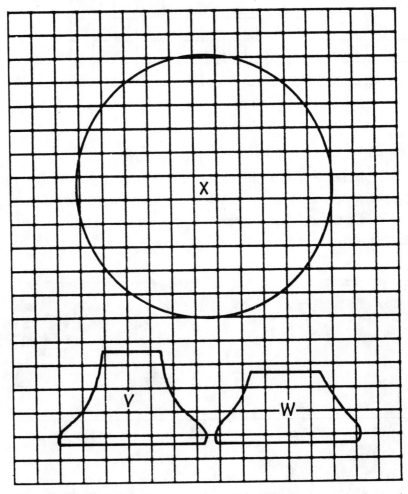

One square = 1" x 1". Number of sections needed: X =1; V=3; W-1.

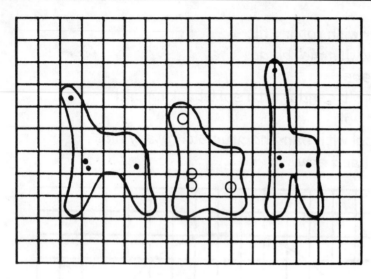

One square = 1" x 1". Circles show where to drill for dowels. Cut two sections for each chain.

Step 1. Trace & cut the project pieces.
Trace patterns on ³/₄-inch birch plywood or ⁵/₄-inch pine. The base pieces must be glued and clamped just like the larger tables. Use a coping saw or a band saw to cut out the sections.

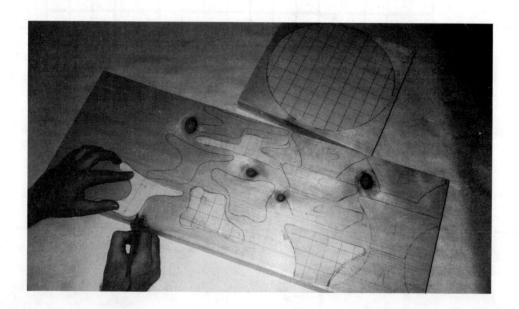

Step 2. Shape the outside of the pieces.

A die grinder works well for shaping the side sections of the chair, as does a Dremel tool (pictured here). However, a mini grinder and 24-grit disc is better for shaping table base.

Step 3. Smooth the pieces.

Use the pneumatic sander or orbital sanders to smooth the pieces. The bicycle pump in the photo is used to inflate the pneumatic sander after changing the sanding sleeves. Sand by hand with 80-grit, then 100-grit sandpaper.

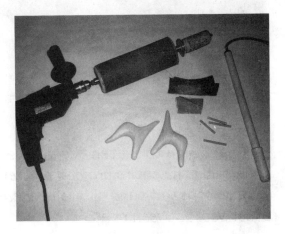

Step 4. Drill the dowel holes.

Use a ¼-inch drill bit to drill the dowel holes, being careful not to drill all the way through the project. Use a coping saw to cut dowels 2½-inch long. Four dowels are used for the chair.

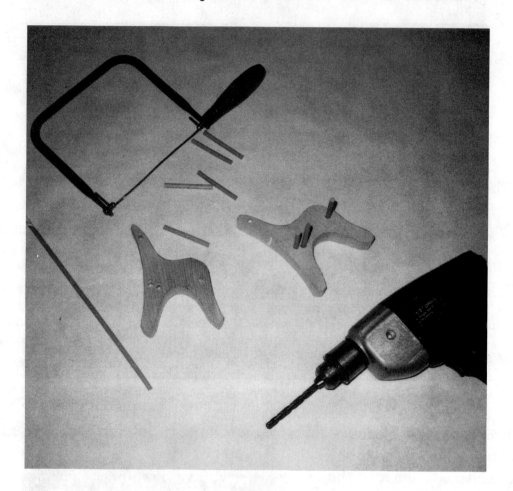

Step 5. Assemble.

Use wood glue to fasten the dowels, then apply a thin coat of tung oil to the entire project and let it dry overnight. At least 2 more coats of tung oil are needed—one coat per day, fine steel wool between coats.

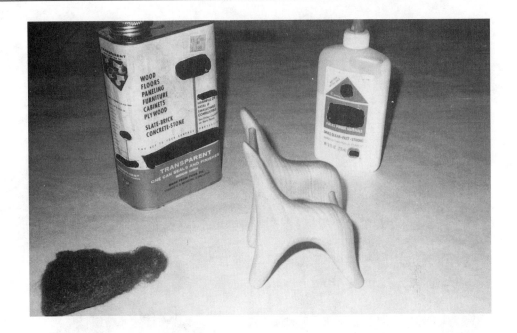

Step 6. Cover the chairs.

To "upholster" cut material, wrap it around the dowels and turn in the frayed edge. Sew the material together on the bottom of seat and behind the backrest by hand.

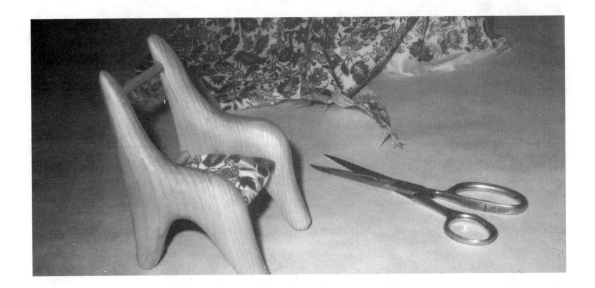

Step 7. Make matching pillows & cushions.

From matching fabric, cut various shapes to be used for
cushions or pillows. These can be sewn with a sewing machine
or by hand.

CHAPTER TEN

Wall vases

These "half" vases can be mounted on a plaque or used directly against the wall. Dried flowers look fantastic in these projects.

WALL VASES

Supplies

¼ sheet 4'-x-5'-x-¾" Finland birch plywood or ¼ sheet 4'-x-5'-x-⅝" Finland birch plywood or 12"-x-12"-x-1" stock in pine cherry, or mahogany

1 8 oz. bottle woodworking glue

1 16- or 24-grit hard-backed sanding disc

1 80- or 100-grit hard-backed sanding disc

1 pkg. ½", ¼", 1" sanding drum sleeves

1 3" sanding sleeve for pneumatic sander, 80- & 100-grit

1 fine- or medium-grit stick-on sanding discs for random orbit or pad sanders

1 pkg. 80-, 150-, 200-grit sandpaper

½ pint oil stain

½ pint tung oil finish

1 extra-fine or steel wool finishing pad

1 quart mineral spirits

2 2" foam brushes

2 pkg. sanding sleeves for Dremel tool

Tools (*indicates optional tool for faster production)

4½" or 5" right-angle mini grinder with flexible backing pad

saber saw with ³⁄₁₆" blade

hand drill with ⅜" chuck

rotary rasp

½", ¾", 1" sanding drums

soft 5" sanding pad

wood file

orbital sander

safety glasses

respirator

scissors
¹⁄₁₆", ⅛", ¼" twist drill
* die grinder with rotary file
* 3" pneumatic sander with 2500 rpm hand drill
* random orbit sander with soft backing pad
* Dremel tool with sanding drums and rotary files
* portable band saw

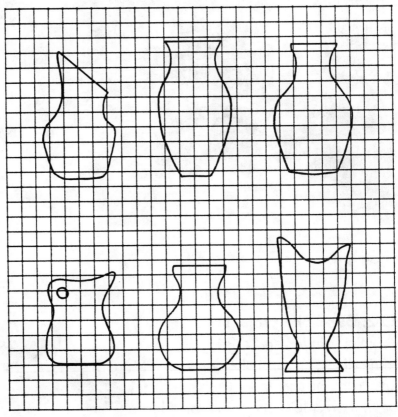

One square = 1" x 1". Cut one section for each vase.

Step 1. Trace & cut out the project.

Trace your favorite shape on a board at least 1 inch thick. Use a portable band saw or coping saw to cut out the project. (Note: As you can see in the project photo, one vase has a hole for a "handle." If you are making this project, drill a ½-inch hole now for the handle.)

Step 2. Sand the project.

Use a mini grinder and a 24-grit sanding disc to round the edge on the front of the vase, then smooth with a 100-grit disc. Sand with a random orbit sander with a 100-grit disc (pictured).

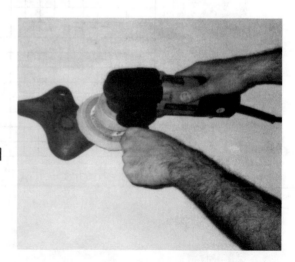

Step 3. Drill a hole for hanging.
Use a hand drill to drill a ⅛-inch hole at 45 degrees in back of vase. Do not go all the way through. A finishing nail hammered into the wall will fit into this hole.

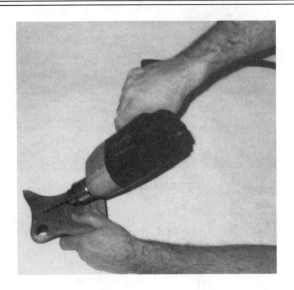

Step 4. Drill holes for holding flowers.
Drill two ½-inch holes about 2 inches deep in the top to hold flowers, then sand with 220-grit paper along the grain.

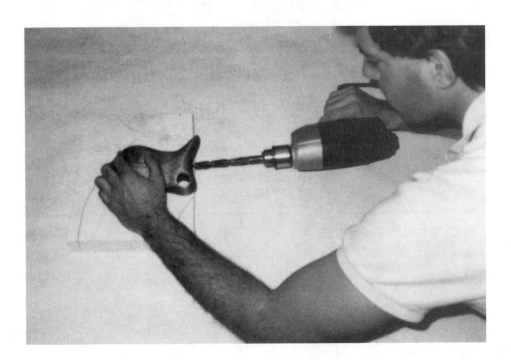

Step 5. Apply a tung oil finish.

Apply a thin coat of tung oil with a brush, and let it dry overnight. The next day, smooth with a fine steel wool or a finishing pad. At least 2 more coats of tung oil are needed— one coat per day, smoothing between coats with fine steel wool.

Step 6. Make a plaque or hang on the wall.

You can glue these vases to a flat piece of wood to make a plaque or hang them directly on the wall.

CHAPTER ELEVEN

Large stool

A large stool is an item that can be useful and will accent any room. The mortise-and-tenon joint used for the rockers (see chapter 3) is also the joint that is used for this project.

LARGE STOOL

Supplies

3 sheets 4'-x-5'-x-¾" Finland birch plywood
1 gallon woodworking glue
4 16- or 24-grit hard-backed sanding discs
2 80- or 100-grit hard-backed sanding discs
10 pkgs. ½", ¼", 1" sanding drum sleeves
2 3" sanding sleeves for pneumatic sander, 80- & 100-grit
2 fine- or medium-grit stick on sanding discs for random
   orbit or pad sanders
5 pkgs. 80-, 150-, 200-grit sandpaper
2 2" foam brushes
5 pkgs. sanding sleeves for dremel tool
1 quart oil stain
1 quart tung oil finish
1 extra-fine steel wool or finishing pad
1 quart mineral spirits

Tools (*indicates optional tool for faster production)

4½" or 5" right-angle mini grinder with flexible backing pad
saber saw with ³⁄₁₆" blade
hand drill with ⅜" chuck
router with template guide & ¼" straight cutter
clamps
rotary rasps
½", ¾", 1" sanding drums
standard ⅜" twist drill
soft 5" sanding pad
staple gun
screwdriver
wood file
orbital sander
safety glasses
respirator
scissors
¹⁄₁₆", ⅛", ¼" twist drill
*Dremel tool with sanding drums & rotary files
*portable band saw
*random orbit sander with soft backing pad
*3" pneumatic sander with 2500 rpm hand drill
*7" right-angle grinder with flexible backing pad
*die grinder with rotary file

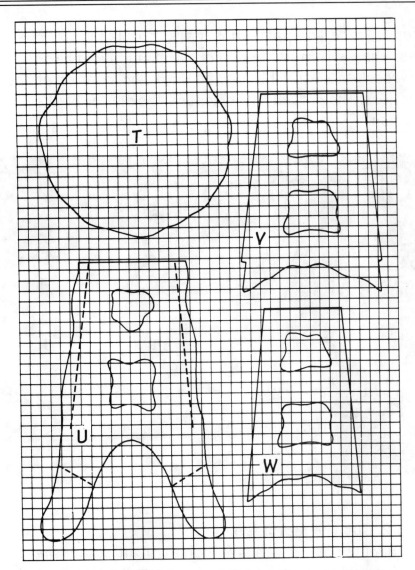

Dotted lines show size & location for 8 laminations for bottom of legs, & center line for mortise cut. One square = 1" x 1". Number of sections needed: T-2; U-6; V-4 (cut 2 without tenons); W-2.

Step 1. Trace the pattern & mark mortises.

Trace the pattern on ⅝-inch or ¾-inch Finland birch plywood. Use a straight edge to mark the location of the mortises. The dotted line indicates the center of the mortise.

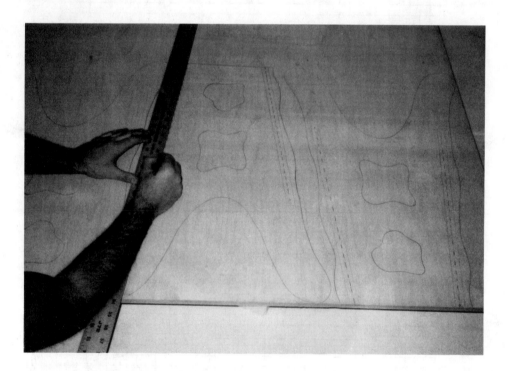

Step 2. Cut the mortises.

Here a router fitted with a ¼-inch straight cutter and a template guide is used to cut the mortises. Use ¼-inch Masonite to make a template for this cut. When using ⅝-inch-thick plywood, cut a straight slot with a saber saw ¹³⁄₁₆-inch wide 16½ inches long—⅞ inch wide if you are using ¾-inch plywood. Center the template over the dotted line and clamp. Cut the mortise ½ inch deep. It is a good idea to try the mortising template on scrap wood first and check for a tight fit with the tenon.

This chair, table, and lamp grouping illustrates the functional use of wood-shaped items.

You don't have to make furniture to use the methods described in this book. This wall vase is an excellent yet decorative alternative to larger pieces.

The unusual design of this "mushroom" table is sure to make it a conversation piece in your home.

Indoors or out, your finished projects will fit with any decor.

If you're inclined to sell your creations, these projects are an excellent choice. Both the adult-size and child-size rockers have sold well, sometimes bringing as much as $2,000!

The projects in this book are not complicated, so children of all ages can participate in the making of unique wooden pieces.

Step 3. Drill holes & cut out sections.

Place pieces of 2-inch thick styrofoam under the plywood
and drill ½-inch holes as guides for the saber saw blade. Stay

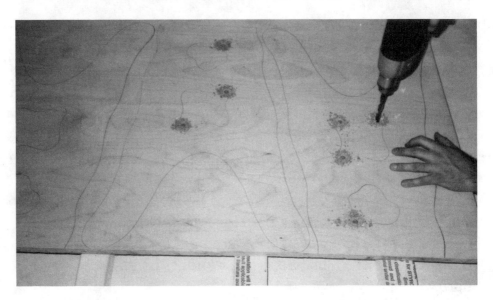

on the inside of lines. Next, use a saber saw to cut out the sections. A blade $^3/_{16}$-inch wide or smaller works well for cutting the straight or curved lines.

Step 4. Apply the glue.

Use a woodworking file to remove any splinters along the edges, and then apply a thin coat of woodworking glue over all surfaces that will come in contact with each other during the lamination stage. You might want too use a staple gun and ½-inch staples to temporarily hold the sections and keep them from slipping.

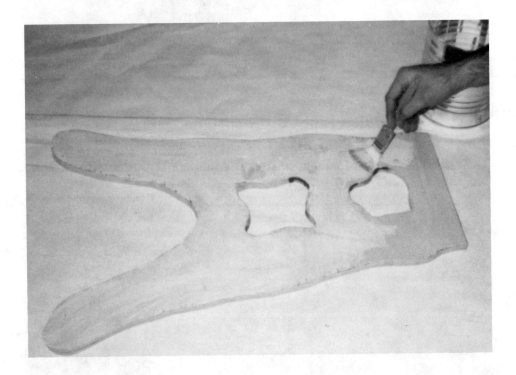

Step 5. Clamp the glued sections together.

Use clamps to apply even pressure all the way around the project. Once the glue has dried, remove the staples with a screwdriver.

Step 6. Shape the project.

Use a right-angle grinder with a 24-grit sanding disc to shape the sections. Use a die grinder with a rotary file around the tight spots, and a 100-grit sanding disc to smooth.

Step 7. Keep the area below the mortises flat.

As with the rockers, the area shown here with dotted lines remains flat. Do not grind away any wood from this area. Also, be sure to keep the bottom of the seat and top of sides flat.

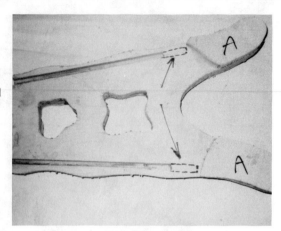

Step 8. Sand the project.

Using a pneumatic sander with an 80-grit sanding sleeve, smooth entire project. Use a drill with drum sanders and the orbital sanders to sand around holes and tight spots. Finally, sand by hand with 220-grit paper.

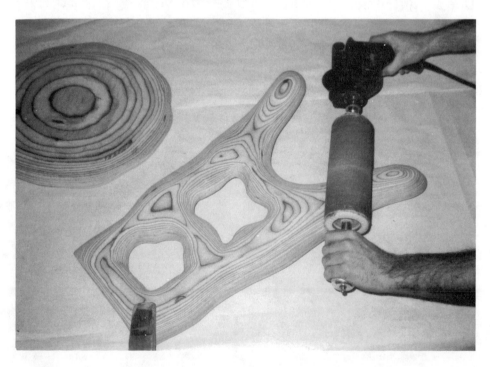

Step 9. Make a trial assembly.

Cut and grind the blocks that will be glued into place to hold seat securely, and make a trial fit. Notice the center mark on the seat. Also notice that the blocks are not square. Use a bevel gauge to check the angle of the blocks for a tight fit.

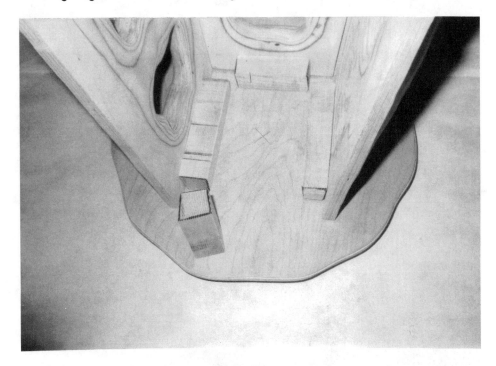

Step 10. Apply a stain.

Use a foam brush to apply oil stain if you want to change the color of the birch plywood. Let this dry overnight.

Step 11. Assemble the project.

Spread woodworking glue along the mortises and tenons and assemble project. Use rope to hold sections in place while the glue is drying.

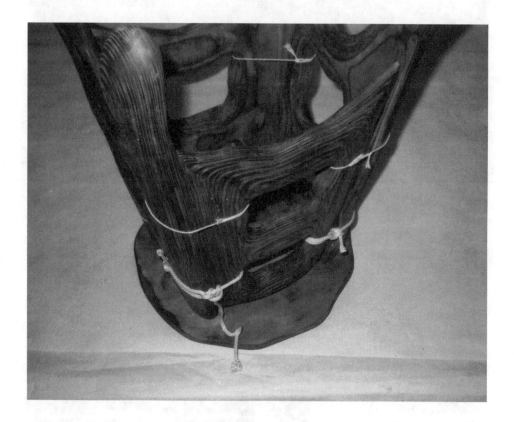

Step 12. Apply the finish.

Brush a thin coat of tung oil on entire project, and let it dry overnight. At least two more coats of tung oil are needed—one coat per day, smoothing with steel wool or finishing pad between coats.

CHAPTER TWELVE

Floor lamp

This floor lamp is not only a very functional project, it is also easy to shape because there are no holes or tight curves.

FLOOR LAMP

Supplies

1 sheet 4'-x-5'-x-¾" (or ⅝") Finland birch plywood
1 gallon woodworking glue
2 16- or 24-grit hard-backed sanding discs
2 80- or 100-grit hard-backed sanding discs
1 3" sanding sleeve for pneumatic sander, 80- & 100-grit
2 fine- or medium-grit stick on sanding discs for random orbit or pad sanders
3 pkgs. 80-, 150-, 200-grit sandpaper
1 quart oil stain
1 pint tung oil finish
1 extra-fine steel wool or finishing pad
1 quart mineral spirits
2 2" foam brushes
1 light-duty extension cord
1 ⅜"-x-2" hollow threaded rod
1 3-way lamp socket
1 3-way light bulb
1 9" harp
1 hardwood knob for finial
1 18" shade

Tools (* indicates optional tool for faster production)
4½" or 5" right-angle mini grinder with flexible backing pad
saber saw with ³⁄₁₆" blade
clamps
18"-x-¾" twist drill
standard ⅜" twist drill
soft 5" sanding pad
heavy-duty staple gun and staples
screwdriver
wire strippers

vise grips
pliers
wood file
orbital sander
safety glasses
respirator
scissors
½" Forstner bit
hammer
* 7" right-angle grinder with flexible backing pad
* 3" pneumatic sander with 2500 rpm hand drill
* random orbit sander with soft backing pad
* portable band saw

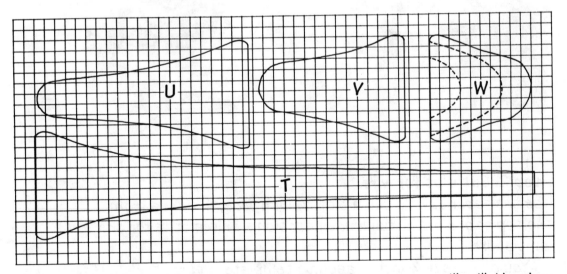

Dotted lines show outer-most laminations. One square = 1" x 1". Number of sections needed: T-5; U-2; V-4; W-4.

Step 1. Trace & cut the pattern.

Trace the pattern onto ¾-inch Finland birch plywood, then place plywood sheet on 2-inch styrofoam. Use a saber saw to cut out sections.

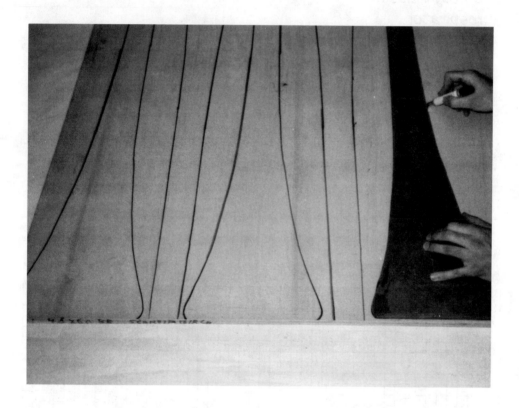

Step 2. Cut slot for wire.

Use the saber saw to cut a slot ¾ inch wide, 4 inches from the top of one of the full length sections. This slot is for the lamp's wire.

You can use a ¼-inch Masonite template and router fitted with a straight cutter and template guide to make the opening for the wire at various depths rather than cutting completely through the section.

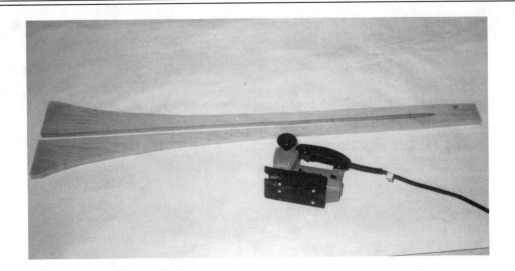

Step 3. Finish the opening.

Use a jig to finish the opening for the wire. Use a ⅜-inch twist drill and an electric hand drill to drill a hole from one edge of a ¾-inch piece of scrap plywood straight through to opposite edge. If you drill through side of block, try it again; the hole must go through center of the block.

Step 4.
Glue another block to the jig.
Use a straightedge to mark the exact center and direction of the hole. Glue another block of ¾-inch plywood on the jig at the end, overlapping pieces by about 4 inches.

Step 5. Mark for wire location.
Mark a straight line in the center of the section from slot to the top. This is where the wire and threaded rod will go through this section. Use a straightedge to line up the line on the jig with the line on the lamp section.

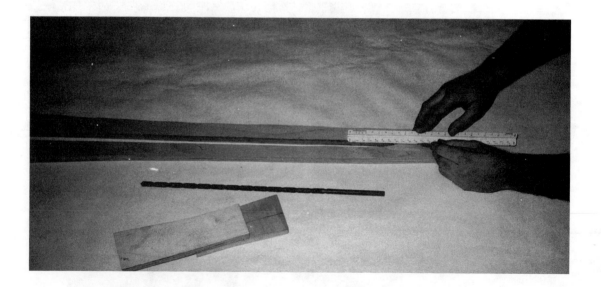

Step 6. Drill the hole for wiring.
Clamp the drilling jig to lamp section securely as shown and use a $\frac{3}{8}$-inch twist drill to drill through the lamp section to the slot.

Step 7.
Glue & clamp sections together.
Spread wood glue over entire surfaces that will come in contact. Use $\frac{1}{2}$-inch staples to hold sections from slipping while glue is drying. Use large handscrew clamps to apply even pressure all the way around each piece. Be sure each section of the lamp is clamped, and allow the glue to dry thoroughly.

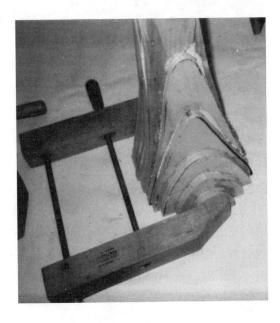

Step 8. Shape the sections.

After you remove the staples with a screwdriver and pliers, use a right-angle grinder with a 24-grit sanding disc to shape the lamp. Smooth with a 100-grit disc. Shown here is an easy way to hold the lamp steady during the grinding process. Clamp two pieces of 2-x-4 on a work table and drill a ½-inch hole high enough for lamp to clear the tabletop. Run metal rods through the wire holes and the 2-x-4. A clamp attached to the lamp keeps the lamp from spinning.

Step 9. Sand the lamp.

Use a pneumatic sander with an 80-grit sleeve to sand the lamp. Sand by hand with 100-grit then 220-grit sandpaper. If you want to change the color of the birch plywood, you should stain the project at this stage and let the stain dry overnight.

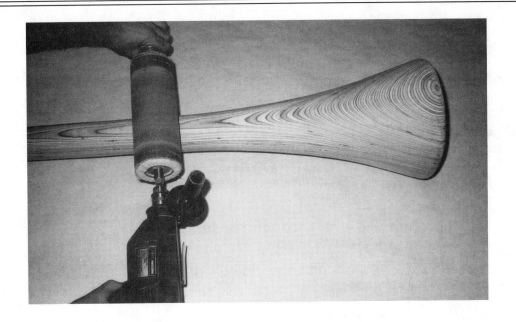

Step 10. Drill the hole for the wire.

Use a ⅜-inch twist drill and an electric hand drill to drill the hole for the wire.

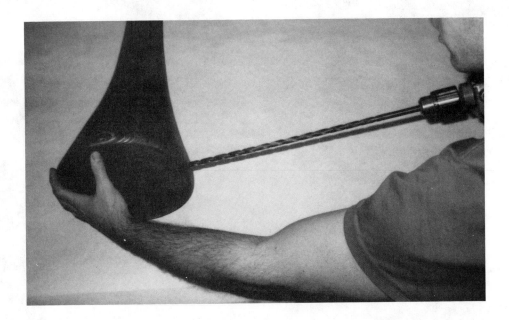

Step 11. Apply finish.

Apply a thin coat of tung oil finish to the entire project, and let it dry overnight. Lightly smooth finish with a finishing pad or fine steel wool. At least two more coats of tung oil are needed—one per day, smoothing between coats with finishing pad or fine steel wool.

Step 12. Run the wire through the lamp.

Cut off the outlets of a light extension cord (15 to 25 feet), and run the end through the side hole and out the bottom. Push a length of string or metal rod through lamp, and attach the wire to the string with tape.

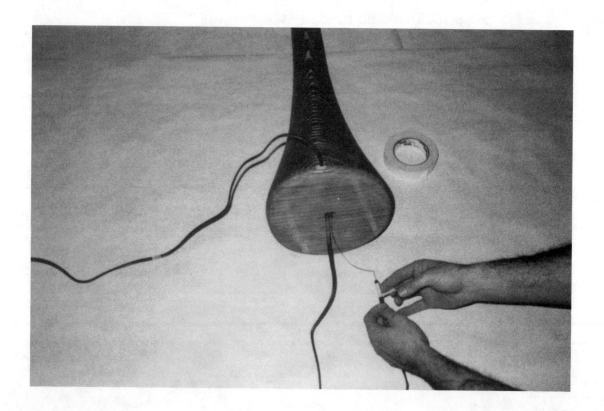

Step 13. Finish wiring the lamp.
Pull the string so the wire snakes through the slot and the ⅜-inch hole. Follow wiring steps from section on making the small table lamps (chapter 13). This lamp will use a 9-inch harp and an 18-inch-x-13-inch lamp shade.

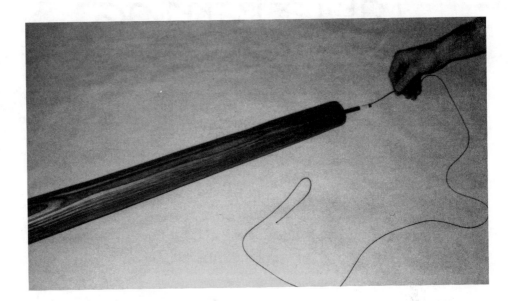

CHAPTER THIRTEEN

Table lamps

Table lamps can be made in varying sizes. The size of the base of the lamp made in this chapter (the middle lamp in the project photo) is 9 inches high and 6 inches across the bottom. A 10-x-7-inch clip-on shade is used, so a harp is not needed. Because you can make lamps of any size simply by enlarging the plans differently, you could create an interesting effect by grouping this lamp with one of another size.

TABLE LAMPS

Supplies

1   sheet 4'-x-5'-x-¾" (or ⅝") Finland birch plywood
1   quart woodworking glue
1   16- or 24-grit hard-backed sanding disc
1   80- or 100-grit hard-backed sanding disc
1   3" sanding sleeve for pneumatic sander, 80- & 100-grit
1   fine- or medium-grit stick on sanding discs for random
    orbit or pad sanders
1   pkg. 80-, 150-, 200-grit sandpaper
1   pint oil stain
1   pint tung oil finish
1   extra-fine steel wool or finishing pad
1   quart mineral spirits
2   2" foam brushes
1   light-duty extension cord
1   ⅜"-x-1½" hollow threaded rod
1   3-way lamp socket
1   3-way light bulb
1   10" clip-on shade

Tools (*indicates optional tool for faster production)
4½" or 5" right-angle mini grinder with flexible backing pad
saber saw with 3/16" blade
hand drill with ⅜" chuck
clamps
18"-x-¾" twist drill
standard ⅜" twist drill
soft 5" sanding pad
heavy-duty staple gun and staples
screwdriver
wire strippers
vise grips

pliers
wood file
orbital sander
safety glasses
respirator
scissors
½" Forstner bit
hammer
* 7" right-angle grinder with flexible backing pad
* 3" pneumatic sander with 2500 rpm hand drill
* random orbit sander with soft backing pad
* portable band saw

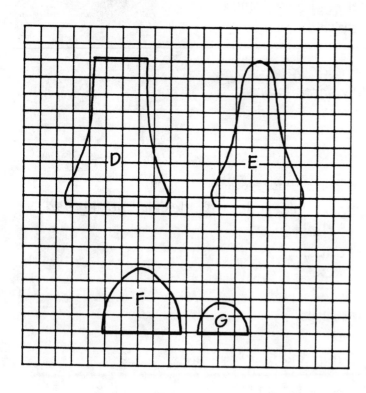

One square = 1" x 1".
Number of sections
needed: D-3; E-2; F-2;
G-2.

Step 1. Trace & cut the pattern.
Trace patterns on ¾-inch birch plywood. Place plywood on 2-inch styrofoam, and use a saber saw to cut the sections down to a manageable size. Then you can easily cut the plywood on the portable band saw. Clamp or bolt saw to your worktable.

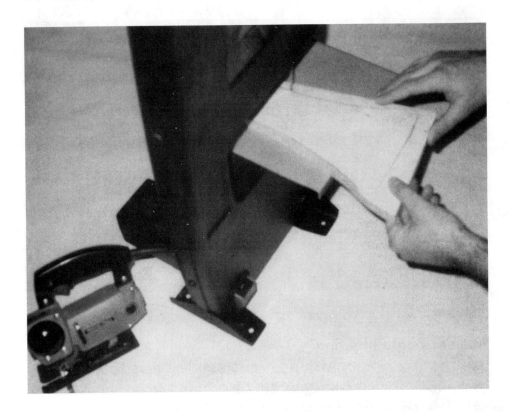

Step 2. Drill a hole for wiring.
Following Steps 2 through 4 in chapter 12, use the same drilling jig to drill a ⅜-inch hole through the middle of one of the full length sections.

Step 3. Glue the sections together overnight.

Spread wood glue on all surfaces that will come in contact.
Use ½-inch staples to hold sections in place while glue is
setting up. (Note: It is easier to remove the staples if they
are not down all the way.) Clamp each section with even
pressure.

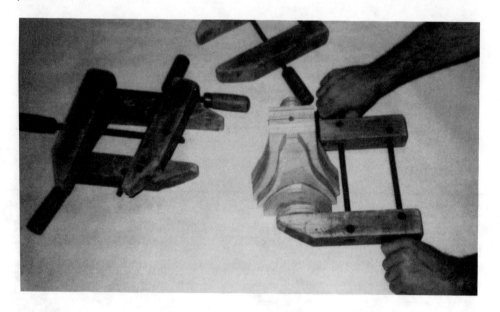

Step 4. Begin shaping.

Use the mini grinder with a 24-grit sanding disc to shape.
Use a 100-grit disc to smooth. Next, use the pneumatic
sander with an 80-grit sleeve then a 100-grit sleeve.

Step 5. Prepare the lamp base for wiring.

With a Forstner bit, enlarge the ⅜-inch hole on the bottom
of the lamp to 1 inch. (Drill 1 inch deep.) Drill an exit hole for
the wire with a ⅜-inch twist drill and an electric hand drill.
The exit hole should be drilled from the back side to the 1-inch
center hole. Make a final sanding with 220-grit sandpaper.

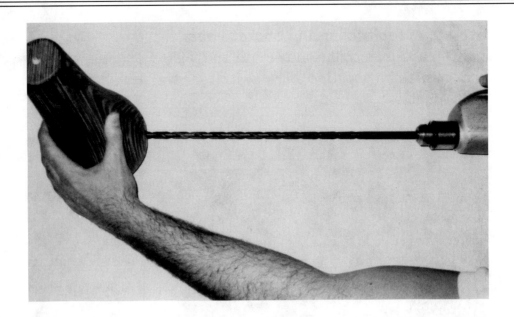

Step 6. Stain & finish the project.

Stain the project with oil stain if you want to change the color of the wood used. Let this dry overnight, then finish with tung oil—at least three coats—one coat per day, smoothing with fine steel wool between coats.

Step 7. Wire the lamp.

Cut off the outlets of a light-duty extension cord, and snake the wire through the base. Slip a 2-inch length of hollow threaded lamp rod over the wire, and turn it clockwise into the 3/8-inch hole. The threads of the lamp rod are protected from the vise grips by two lamp nuts tightened back-to-back on the rod. Leave 3/4-inch of the rod above the base.

Step 8. Attach collar and socket base.
Tighten a ½-inch collar on the rod and then a standard socket base on top. Use a line switch for the 4-inch night light (right).

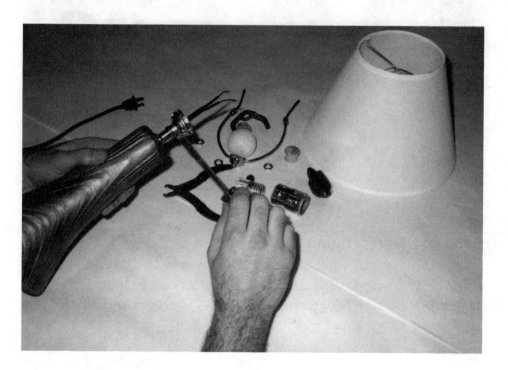

Step 9. Complete wiring.
Use wire strippers to remove a ½-inch piece of insulation from the end of the extension cord. The socket has two connecting screws—one for each half of the extension cord wire. Hook the bare wire over these screws and tighten the screws with a screwdriver. Attach the conductor with a white or other identifying rib to the silver-colored screw and the other to the brass-colored screw. Wrap the wire counterclockwise under head of screw and tighten screw clockwise. Cut off excess copper strands.

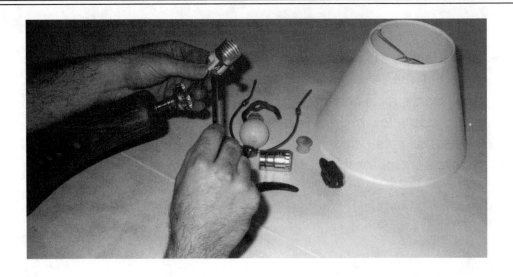

Step 10. Assemble the lamp.
Slip the cardboard insulation over the socket, then the metal shell. The shell will snap into place when it is all the way down. Have the switch facing the front of the lamp.

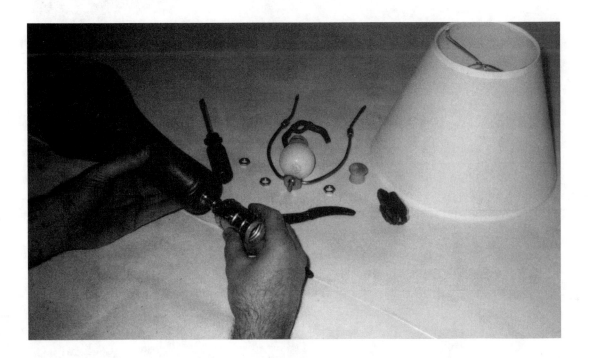

Note: While this particular lamp does not require one, the larger lamps will need a harp to hold the shade. The harp base goes between the collar and socket and is held secure with two lamp nuts. For the smaller lamps, use a clip-on shade.

Do not allow children to wire lamps. Have all wiring inspected by an electrician. Make sure wire is unplugged before cutting or wiring lamp.

CHAPTER FOURTEEN

Chair

While this chair is a beautiful piece when the seat and the backrest are made the same way as the rockers, an alternative to sculpting is to have the seat and backrest professionally upholstered with foam rubber and heavy cloth. For those of you who would like to try your hand at upholstery, brief directions on how to cover the chair yourself are included at the end of this chapter. The wood sections for the seat and backrest are very easy to make when you plan to upholster them because no laminating or grinding is necessary. Either way, this chair, as shown on page 128, will be a unique addition to any room.

CHAIR

Supplies

5 sheets 4'-x-5'-x-⅝" (or ¾") Finland birch plywood
1 gallon woodworking glue
4 16- or 24-grit hard-backed sanding discs
2 80- or 100-grit hard-backed sanding discs
5 pkgs. of ½", ¼", 1" sanding drum sleeves
2 3" sanding sleeves, 80- or 100-grit
2 fine or medium grit sticks on sanding discs for random orbit or pad sanders
3 pkgs. of 80-, 150-, 200-grit sandpaper
2 quarts oil stain
1 quart tung oil finish
1 fine steel wool or finishing pad
1 quart of mineral spirits (for cleaning)
2 2" foam brushes
1 box upholstery tacks
1 foam bed pad
1 high-density camping pad
1 piece 3'-x-8' upholstery fabric

Tools (*indicates optional tool for faster production)
4½" or 5" right-angle mini grinder
saber saw with ³⁄₁₆" blade
hand drill with ⅜" chuck
router with template guide & ¼" straight cutter
clamps
rotary rasps
½", ¾", 1" sanding drums
standard ⅜" twist drill
soft 5" sanding pad
heavy-duty staple gun & staples
hammer

screwdriver
wood file
orbital sander
safety glasses
respirator
scissors
hammer
* 7" right-angle grinder with flexible backing pad
* die grinder with rotary file
* 3" pneumatic sander with 2500 rpm hand drill
* Dremel tool with sanding drums & rotary files
* random orbit sander with soft backing pad
* portable band saw

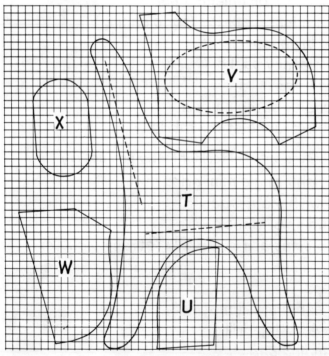

Dotted lines show location of seat & backrest mortise. One square = 1" x 1". Number of sections needed: T-6; U-2; V-2; W-2; X-2.

Step 1. Trace the pattern.

Trace the pattern on ⅝-inch or ¾-inch Finland birch plywood. The circles on the template show where 4 holes have been drilled. Put a pencil point through these holes and mark the plywood. Use a straightedge to connect the dots (dotted line).

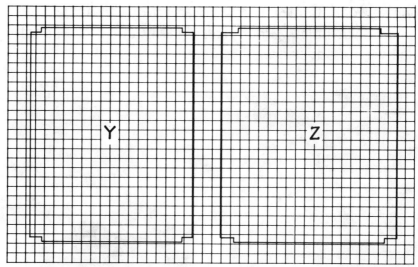

One square = 1" x 1". Cut one section for each (Y & Z).

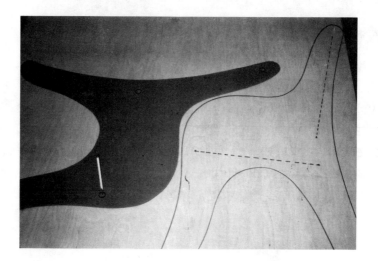

Step 2. Cut the mortises and the sections.

Here a router fitted with a ¼-inch straight cutter and a template guide is used to cut the mortises. Use ¼-inch Masonite to make a template for this cut, or use the rocker's mortising template, as I am doing here. When using ⅝-inch-thick plywood, cut a straight slot with a saber saw $^{13}/_{16}$ inch wide by length of mortise—⅞ inch wide if you are using ¾-inch plywood. Center the template over the dotted line and clamp. Cut holes ½ inch deep. Finally, cut out all sections of chair with a saber saw.

Step 3. Glue sections together.

Remove any splinters with a file, and then spread glue evenly over all surfaces that will come in contact. Use a staple gun and ½" staples to keep section in place while glue is drying. Use clamps to apply even pressure all the way around project on each section. Let glue dry thoroughly.

Step 4. Begin shaping.

After you have removed the staples with a screwdriver and pliers, use the right-angle grinders to shape the sides of the chair. Use a 24-grit sanding disc for roughing out, then a 100-grit for smoothing.

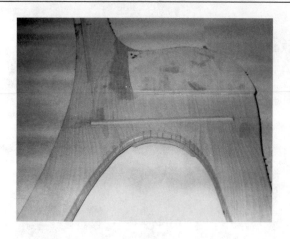

Step 5.
Sand carefully around mortises.
As with the rockers and stool, do not use grinders around the mortises where seat and backrest touch sides.

Step 6. Sand & stain the project.
Use the pneumatic sander and the orbital sanders to smooth. Use 80-grit, then 100-grit sandpaper. Sand by hand with 220-grit sandpaper. Remove sawdust, then brush on oil stain if you want to change the color of birch.

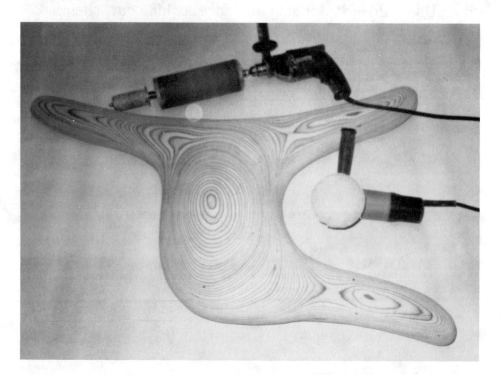

Step 7. Glue the sections in place.

Apply woodworking glue along mortises and tenons. Assemble, then hold the sections together with rope. Allow glue to dry for at least three hours.

Upholstering Your Chair

Cut, with scissors, ½-inch high-density foam rubber (such as a backpacking sleeping pad) to fit between side sections. Staple this along the edge with ⅜-inch staples.

Cut 1 inch of low-density foam (such as a mattress pad) to fit between the side sections. Again, to hold it in place, staple along the edge with ⅜-inch staples.

Fold your upholstery material under along the edge, then staple it into place. Also use upholstery tacks to secure the material. Sew the seam on the bottom and back where the ends of the material meet, then use a strip of the same color material to cover the tacks along the edge.

CHAPTER FIFTEEN

Mushroom table

You can use a mushroom table as a platform for potted plants, a stool, or child's work surface. For the following sequence, I used 1¼-inch pine.

MUSHROOM TABLE

Supplies

1   sheet 16"-x-13'-1' stock (pine, cherry, butternut, walnut,
      etc.) or 1 sheet 4'-x-5'-x-$\frac{3}{4}$" (or $\frac{5}{8}$") Finland birch plywood
1   quart woodworking glue
1   16- or 24-grit hard-backed sanding disc
1   80- or 100-grit hard-backed sanding disc
1   3" sanding sleeve for pneumatic sander, 80- & 100-grit
1   fine- or medium-grit stick on sanding discs for random
      orbit or pad sanders
1   pkg. 80-, 150-, 200-grit sandpaper
2   2" foam brushes
1   pint oil stain
1   pint tung oil finish
1   extra-fine steel wool or finishing pad
1   quart mineral spirits
1   2$\frac{1}{4}$"-x-$\frac{1}{4}$" dowel screw

Tools (*indicates optional tool for faster production)
4$\frac{1}{2}$" or 5" right-angle mini grinder with flexible backing pad
saber saw with $\frac{3}{16}$" wide blade
hand drill with $\frac{3}{8}$" chuck
clamps
standard $\frac{3}{8}$" twist drill
soft 5" sanding pad
heavy-duty staple gun & staples
screwdriver
vise grips
pliers
wood file
orbital sander
safety glasses
respirator

scissors
¹⁄₁₆", ¹⁄₈", ¹⁄₄" twist drill
*7" right-angle grinder with flexible backing pad
*3" pneumatic sander with 2500 rpm hand drill
*random orbit sander with soft backing pad
*portable band saw

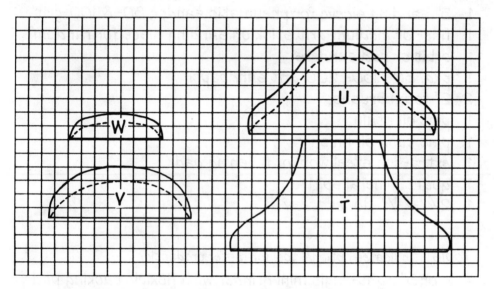

One square = 1" x 1". Number of sections needed: T-10; U-6;
V-4; W-4. (Note: Cut 3 sections of top only if 2-inch wood is
used.)

Step 1. Trace and cut the pattern.

Trace the patterns. Line up the bottom of pattern with the
edge of the board. Use 2-inch-thick wood or glue two pieces
of 1¼-inch wood together for the tabletop. Tabletop is 16" in
diameter. Place the board on pieces of 2-inch styrofoam. Cut
out sections with a saber saw.

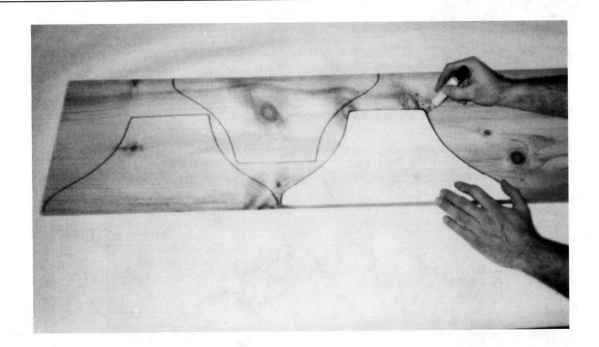

Step 2.
Glue & secure sections together.
Spread glue over all surfaces that will come in contact. Here I am using a plastic glue dispenser with a roller attached. Next, staple sections together with ½-inch staples to keep them from slipping during the clamping stage. Do not allow staples to go all the way down; it will make removing them difficult. Use large hand screw clamps to apply even pressure on each section of project.

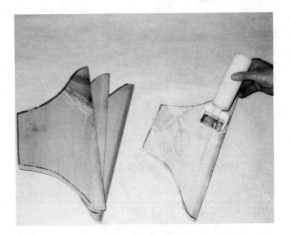

Step 3. Begin shaping.

Remove staples with a screwdriver, then use a mini grinder and a 24-grit grinding disc to shape the base and tabletop with a 100-grit disc. (Do not shape the top of the base or the bottom of the tabletop.) Use sanders to smooth.

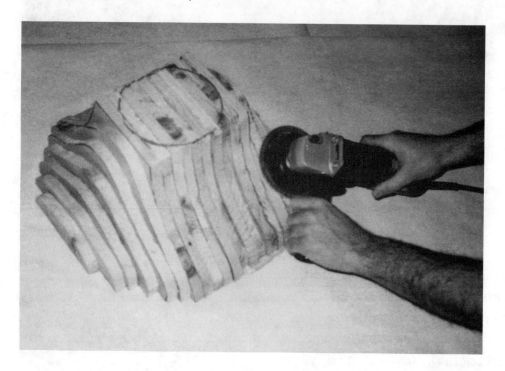

Step 4.
Drill holes in the base & top.

Drill ⅛-inch holes in the middle of the base and in the top, 1 inch deep in both sections. Use tape on the drill as a guide to prevent drilling too deep in the top. Next, use vise grips to screw in a 2-inch-x-¼-inch furniture screw.

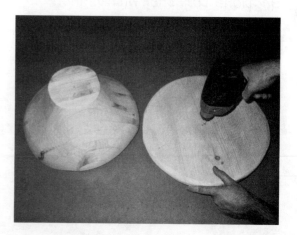

Step 5.
Attach the top to the base.
Apply a thin coat of glue around the top of base and bottom of table where pieces come in contact. Screw on the tabletop until it sits tight against the base.

Step 6. Stain & finish the project.
Stain the project or finish with tung oil. If it will be used outside or with plants, use exterior polyurethane for the finish. Use four or five coats, one coat per day.

CHAPTER SIXTEEN

Plant holder

This project is fastened to a wall and filled with plants. To protect the piece, you must use a plastic or glass tray on the inside if live plants are going to be watered.

PLANT HOLDER

Supplies

¼ sheet 4'-x-5'-x-⅝" (or ¾") Finland birch plywood
¼ sheet 4'-x-5'-x-¼" Finland birch plywood
1 quart woodworking glue
1 16- or 24-grit hard-backed sanding disc
1 80- or 100-grit hard-backed sanding disc
3 pkg. ½", ¼", 1" sanding drum sleeves
1 3" sanding sleeve for pneumatic sander, 80- & 100-grit
1 fine- or medium-grit stick on sanding discs for random orbit or pad sanders
1 pkg. 80-, 150-, 200-grit sandpaper
2 2" foam brushes
½ pint oil stain
½ pint tung oil finish
1 extra-fine steel wool or finishing pad
1 quart mineral spirits

Tools (*indicates optional tool for faster production)

4½" or 5" right-angle mini grinder with flexible backing pad
saber saw with ³⁄₁₆" wide blade
hand drill with ⅜" chuck
rotary rasps
½", ¾", 1" sanding drums
soft 5" sanding pad
heavy-duty staple gun & staples
screwdriver
wood file
orbital sander
safety glasses
respirator
scissors
¹⁄₁₆", ⅛", ¼" twist drill

* die grinder with rotary file
* 3" pneumatic sander with 2500 rpm hand drill
* random orbit sander with soft backing pad
* Dremel tool with sanding drums & rotary files
* portable band saw

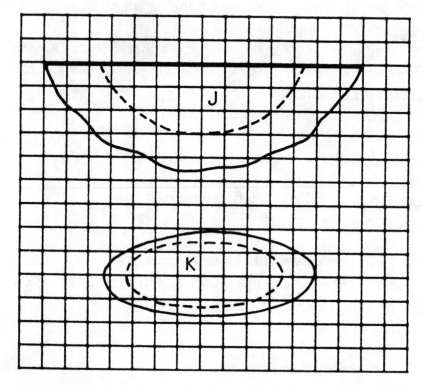

One square = 1" x 1". Cut 9 sections of J, 5 along dotted line. Cut 2 sections of K.

Step 1. Trace & cut patterns.
Trace patterns on ⅝-inch or ¾-inch birch plywood. The back piece is cut from ¼-inch birch plywood. Five pieces have U-shapes cut in them to eliminate much of the grinding on the inside of the planter (see top of photo).

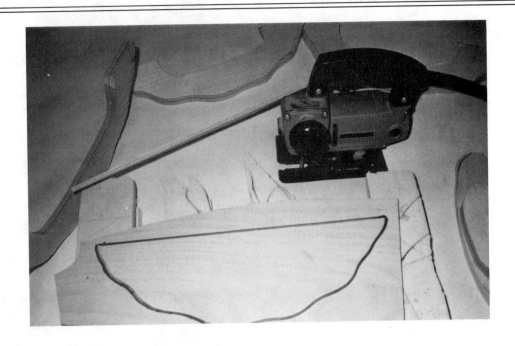

Step 2. Glue & clamp sections together.

Use wood glue on all sections that will come in contact. Do not glue the 1/4-inch piece on back at this time, or it will be

too difficult to shape inside of planter. Use ½-inch staples to hold sections in place during clamping. Staples should stick up a little to make removing them easy. Clamp all sections with even pressure, and let the project dry for at least one hour.

Step 3. Begin shaping.
Remove staples with a screwdriver and pliers. Use a mini grinder and a 24-grit sanding disc to shape the outside. Smooth with a 100-grit disc.

Step 4. Smooth the project.
As shown, use a die grinder with a rotary file to shape the inside. Then use a pneumatic sander or orbital sanders to smooth. Use 80-grit paper, then 100-grit paper.

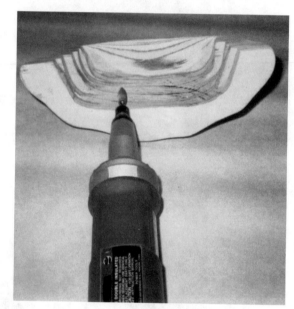

Step 5. Attach the back.
Use wood glue to attach ¼-inch back. Clamp in place until the glue is dry, then grind and sand the ¼-inch back until it is flush with sides of the planter.

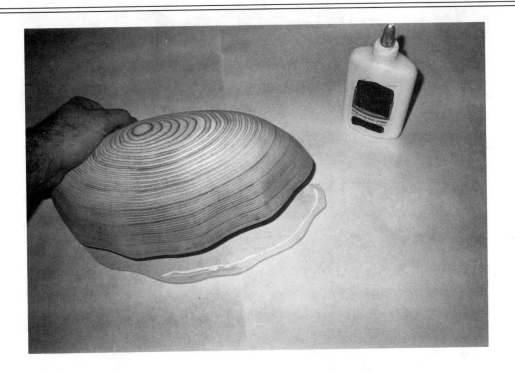

Step 6. Stain & finish the project.

Stain the project, if desired, and finish with tung oil—at least three coats—one coat per day, smoothing with steel wool between coats. Use a ⅛-inch drill to drill a hole to hang.

CHAPTER SEVENTEEN

Large vase

A large vase such as this one is ideal for dried flowers, but you could use it for live plants if you fit it with a plastic or glass liner.

LARGE VASE

Supplies

½ sheet 4'-x-5'-x-⅝" (or ¾") Finland birch plywood or 6"-x-10"-x-1" stock (pine, cherry, butternut, walnut, etc.)

1 quart woodworking glue

1 16- or 24-grit hard-backed sanding disc

1 80- or 100-grit hard-backed sanding disc

2 pkgs. ½", ¼", 1" sanding drum sleeves

1 3" sanding sleeve for pneumatic sander, 80- & 100-grit

1 fine- or medium-grit stick on sanding discs for random orbit or pad sanders

1 pkg. 80-, 150-, 200-grit sandpaper

2 2" foam brushes

1 pint oil stain

½ pint tung oil finish

1 extra-fine steel wool or finishing pad

1 quart mineral spirits

Tools (*indicates optional tool for faster production)

4½" or 5" right-angle mini grinder with flexible backing pad

saber saw with ³⁄₁₆" wide blade

hand drill with ⅜" chuck

clamps

rotary rasps

½", ¾", 1" sanding drums

standard ⅜" twist drill

soft 5" sanding pad

heavy-duty staple gun & staples

screwdriver

wood file

orbital sander

safety glasses

respirator

scissors
¹⁄₁₆", ⅛", ¼" twist drill
* 3" pneumatic sander with 2500 rpm hand drill
* 18"-x-⅜" twist drill
* random orbit sander with soft backing pad
* portable band saw

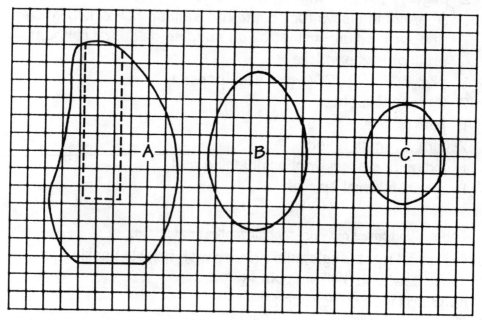

One square = 1" x 1". Dotted line shows where to hollow out vase. Number of sections needed: A-6; B-2; C-2.

Step 1. Trace & cut the pattern.
Trace pattern on ¾-inch or ⅝-inch Finland birch plywood. Place the plywood on 2-inch-thick styrofoam. Use a saber saw to cut out sections.

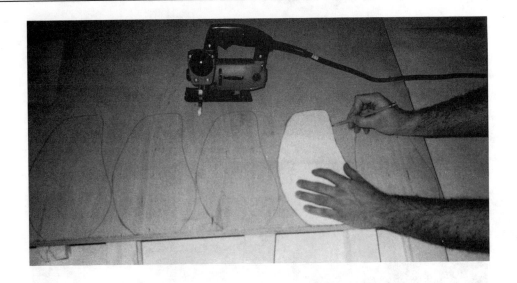

Step 2. Glue & clamp the sections.

Divide the sections into two groups and clamp the two piles separately. Use wood glue and hand-screw clamps to apply even pressure on each piece.

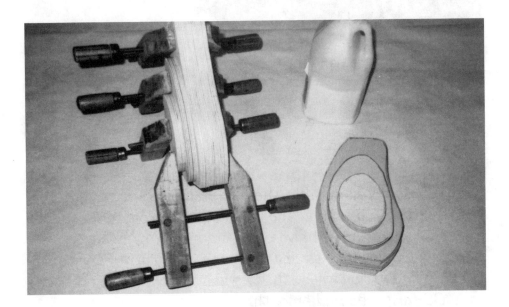

Step 3. Begin shaping.

Use a mini grinder and a 24-grit sanding disc to hollow out the center of the vase and to shape outside (shown here). Use a 100-grit disc to smooth the outside and a random orbit sander with 80-grit paper to smooth the inside.

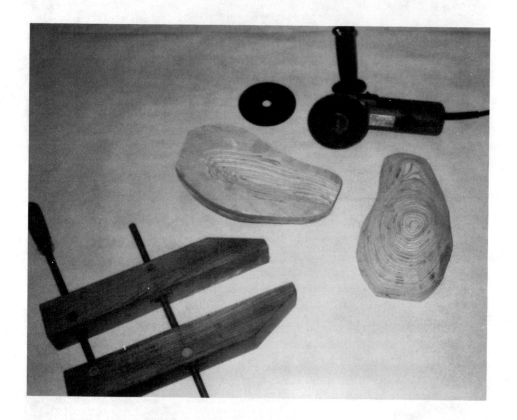

Step 4. Glue & assemble the two halves.

Spread wood glue around the hollowed-out area on the inside of vase. Assemble the halves, and clamp them together tightly. Allow the glue to dry, then use the mini grinder to even up the section where the two halves were joined. Switch to a 100- grit disc and smooth.

Step 5. Sand to smooth.
Use electric sanders to smooth further—first using 80-grit, then 100-grit sandpaper. Make a final sanding by hand with 220-grit sandpaper.

Step 6. Apply finish.
Apply oil stain with a brush if you care to change the color of the wood. Finish with three or four coats of tung oil—one coat per day, smoothing with fine steel wool between coats.

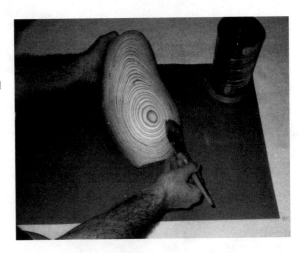

Glossary

airfoil an airplane wing, propeller blade, or other similar shapes.

backing pad a hard or soft disc used to hold sandpaper on grinding discs when attached to a power tool.

band saw a power saw fitted with a blade that is in the form of an endless steel belt.

bevel gauge an instrument consisting of two arms joined together and opening to any angle for drawing angles or adjusting saw blades to a desired angle.

binding pins threaded metal pins used to hold pages of accounting books or albums together.

boat patches thin, boat-shaped pieces of wood used to fill voids in plywood.

boomerang an airfoil designed to return when thrown by hand.

carbide a very hard metal made of carbon and one or more heavy metals.

center punch metal tool used to drive nails below the surface of wood when struck with a hammer.

chisel metal tool with a cutting edge used to shape a solid material.

chuck a device for holding a rotating tool or workpiece during an operation.

chuck key used to tighten a chuck.

coping saw a hand saw with a narrow blade used to cut curved shapes.

countersink a hole cut to accept the head of a screw or bolt below the surface of the work being fastened.

Dremel tool an electric tool that is fitted with interchangeable cutting heads connected to a flexible shaft.

diameter distance across the widest points of a circle.

die grinder high-speed electric tool that is fitted with a cutter to shape or smooth solid material.

dowel a round shaft of wood, cut to a precise diameter.

dowel screw special screw used to fasten sections of furniture, sometimes referred to as a furniture screw.

drill gauge attachment a tool used to steady a hand drill at a preset angle.

drum sander a sander that is fitted with sanding sleeves and is turned by an electric power tool.

dust mask mask worn on the face to keep dust from entering the mouth and nose.

enamel paint smooth paint that dries with a glossy appearance.

epoxy very strong, two-part adhesive used to adhere metal, plastic, wood, etc.

extension cord insulated wire with a plug at one end and an outlet at the other end.

file metal tool with multiple cutting edges used to smooth or shape a solid material.

finial decorative knob used to hold a lamp shade on the lamp's harp.

finishing nail narrow nail with a small head.

finishing pad hard plastic pad used to smooth finish between coats.

Forstner bit drill bit used to cut holes with a flat bottom.

GFCI (ground fault circuit interrupter) A safety device designed to eliminate an electrical shock.

grain the direction, size, arrangement, and appearance of the fibers in wood.

graphite paper paper used when tracing designs, letters, etc., to transfer to another surface.

grid pattern series of identical squares (ex: graph paper).

hand screw clamps woodworking clamp consisting of two hardwood jaws and two threaded rods for tightening.

harp loop of metal used to hold a lamp shade over the socket and bulb.

jig device that holds the work and/or guides a tool while forming or assembling wood parts.

joint the area where ends or edges of two boards are attached.

laminate to form a product by bonding together two or more layers of material; each layer is called a lamination or ply.

lamp socket lamp part that is wired and holds the light bulb.

Masonite dark brown fiberboard that can be cut and shaped with woodworking tools.

mineral spirits petroleum product used for thinning paint and finishes or for cleaning brushes.

mini grinder an abbreviated name for a high-speed right-angle grinder.

model representation of product usually made of an inexpensive material during the designing stages of a new product.

mortise a hole, groove, or slot cut into wood to receive a tenon when making a joint.

oil stain   product used for changing the natural color of wood.

orbital sander   sander that vibrates the sandpaper with a circular motion.

pattern   paper cutout used to trace exact shape and size of project to wood.

pilot hole   hole drilled to accept the threaded part of a screw.

plan   drawing showing the size and shape of a woodworking project.

plywood   material consisting of thin sheets of wood glued together with the grain of adjacent layers laminated at right angles.

pneumatic   pertaining to or operated by air pressure.

polyurethane   plastic-based wood finish.

random orbit sander   a disc finishing sander designed to smooth wood without leaving scratch marks.

rasp   woodworking file with large teeth for removing wood fast.

ratchet wrench   a wrench consisting of a toothed wheel and saw that allows effective motion in one direction only; to tighten or loosen screws, nuts, and bolts.

respirator   object worn over the mouth and nose to prevent sawdust from entering respiratory tract.

right angle grinder   electric disc grinder used to grind weld metal or wood. Can also be fitted with sanding discs for smoothing wood.

rotary file   revolving cutting head used in a die grinder to shape and smooth wood.

rough-cut lumber   boards that have not been planed smooth.

router   machine with a revolving vertical spindle and cutter for milling out the surface of wood.

router bit interchangeable cutting head for making decorative edges on boards, trimming, or milling.

rpm abbreviation for *revolutions per minute.*

saber saw light, portable, electric saw with a pointed reciprocating blade.

sanding disc paper or fiber disc used to smooth wood when attached to a power tool, available in various grits from fine to course.

sanding sleeve paper or cloth cylinder used to smooth wood when attached to power tool, available in various grits from fine to course.

sculpt to remove material to form a desired shape or design.

shank hole hole drilled to accept the threadless part of a screw.

speed bore drill tool used for drilling large holes with an electric drill with a small chuck opening.

steel wool an abrasive material composed of long, fine steel shavings and used for smoothing finishes between coats.

straightedge a straight strip of wood or metal used to lay out and check the accuracy of work.

styrofoam expanded rigid polystyrene plastic.

surform tool small hand tool used to shape wood or auto body filler.

taper a gradual and uniform decrease in the size of a hole, cylinder, or rectangular part.

template a pattern or guide that is used to lay out work or check its accuracy.

template guide router accessory used to follow around a thin template during the cutting process.

tenon projecting edge of a board that fits into a groove or slot (mortise) on another piece.

threaded rod hollow metal rod with exterior threads used to hold a lamp socket on the lamp's base.

twist drill drill with a spiral shaped cutting edge.

upholstery materials like fabric or padding used to make a soft covering for a seat.

upholstery tacks short nails used to hold upholstery permanently in place.

vise grip pliers pliers that can be adjusted to lock onto the work tightly.

washer flat, donut-shaped pieces of metal used in conjunction with bolts and nuts.

wing nut threaded nut with wing-shaped knobs for adjusting by hand.

Index